Waking Up an Empath

A Year in the Life
of an Empath
from Awakening
to Spiritual Healer

Kim Wuirch

BALBOA
PRESS

A DIVISION OF HAY HOUSE

Balboa Press books may be ordered through booksellers or by contacting:

Balboa Press
A Division of Hay House
1663 Liberty Drive
Bloomington, IN 47403
www.balboapress.com
1 (877) 407-4847

Print information available on the last page.

ISBN: 978-1-5043-7168-1 (sc)
ISBN: 978-1-5043-7169-8 (hc)
ISBN: 978-1-5043-7181-0 (e)

Library of Congress Control Number: 2016920717

Balboa Press rev. date: 12/28/2016

DEDICATION

*I dedicate this book to my son Seth, and my mom
who supported and loved me unconditionally.*

*A special thanks to all my friends who stood by my side
through all the weirdness, and still called me a friend.*

ACKNOWLEDGEMENTS

To my instructors and guides here on earth,
Thank you for sharing your wisdom,
Your love and your patience.

To my Angels and Archangels
Your advice while sometimes hard to understand
Was always welcome and appreciated.

To my editor Keidi Keating and Your Book Angel
You truly were my book angel.

To my partner Ken Lewicki
Who gave me the confidence to publish this book.

AUTHOR'S NOTE

This book is NOT based on scientific facts or years of research. It's simply based on my own personal experience and spiritual growth. When going through a spiritual awakening, no one has the luxury of knowing all the answers. We are not supposed to know everything. Instead, we each go through a period of growth, physically, mentally, emotionally, and spiritually. The key is learning to use your intuition and insight. That's how you learn to rely on that inner voice, which **always** has the right answers for YOU. Critics and naysayers may say I'm wrong and that's fine. Everyone is entitled to their opinion. I'm not asking anyone to believe me. If this book is meant for you to read, it will find its way to you. If you are meant to understand then you will. If this book is meant to lead you to me then I will welcome you.

It is my hope and dream that by sharing my own personal experiences, maybe I can help someone else through their spiritual transition. It will not be the same as mine. But rather I hope my thought process shows you there are always answers if you seek them. There is always help if you ask for it. There are others like you out there if only you look. I ask that you don't simply sit back and let life happen to you. Instead, I encourage you to take charge of it. I shared my sources of aid and guidance not as a reference, but to show you there are options, and if I can find them, anyone can.

Not everything you read in this book will resonate with you and that's okay. Maybe some of it will or perhaps none of it will. The underlying message is that I have experienced the confusion and turmoil of sudden spiritual awareness and I hope by reading this book, your awakening will be a little smoother.

Most of the names in this book have been changed. The real names that remain, I want to personally thank them for giving their permission to be cited in my book.

May peace find you and be with you always.

Kim Wuirch

CONTENTS

EMPATH QUIZ

Using a pencil circle Agree, Disagree or Unsure for each question.

1.	You can influence the moods of those around you.	Agree Disagree Unsure
2.	Plants and animals have consciousness.	Agree Disagree Unsure
3.	Children often stare at you.	Agree Disagree Unsure
4.	Strangers tell you very personal things about themselves.	Agree Disagree Unsure
5.	You feel rejuvenated after being outdoors or gardening.	Agree Disagree Unsure
6.	You cry easily sometimes for no reason.	Agree Disagree Unsure
7.	You get overwhelmed in crowded places.	Agree Disagree Unsure

8. You have always been told you were sensitive.	Agree Disagree Unsure
9. You know things but cannot explain how you know.	Agree Disagree Unsure
10. Mood swings are not uncommon for you.	Agree Disagree Unsure
11. You suspect you are a human lie detector.	Agree Disagree Unsure
12. You can physically feel another person's pain or suffering.	Agree Disagree Unsure
13. You avoid malls or large shopping centers.	Agree Disagree Unsure
14. You cannot watch the news without becoming depressed the remainder of the day.	Agree Disagree Unsure
15. Violence towards others is unfathomable to you.	Agree Disagree Unsure
16. Friends and strangers share their deepest secrets with you but you didn't ask.	Agree Disagree Unsure
17. You know someone's mood even when they try to hide it.	Agree Disagree Unsure
18. You have a hyper sensitive sense of smell and strong scents can over power you.	Agree Disagree Unsure

19. Your emotions change quickly around other people.	Agree Disagree Unsure
20. You avoid conflict at all costs.	Agree Disagree Unsure
21. You do not like strangers standing close to you, so line ups are very uncomfortable.	Agree Disagree Unsure
22. Being a day dreamer is just who you are.	Agree Disagree Unsure
23. Rough clothing, tags and abrasive material are unbearable against your skin.	Agree Disagree Unsure
24. You can feel people even when they are not touching you.	Agree Disagree Unsure

If you agreed to 15 or more of these questions, *you are an empath*.

EMPATH SYMBOL

The Empath Symbol has been provided by the Symbols Archangel and for the first time ever, introduced to the human race.

Enter into new possibilities with this empath symbol. Let it take you to new heights of spiritual development. Step into your power with increased strength and awareness of the spirit realm. Through the use of this symbol you can increase your spiritual communication, enhance abilities and become more heart centered, loving and at peace.

Recommendations for how to use this symbol:

~ Use it to identify those who are awakened by wearing the symbol or having it near you in some form.

~ Draw it in the air with your hands.

~ Put the symbol on your glass or bottle of water to change the molecular structure of the water.

*This symbol is intended for personal use only.

CHAPTER 1

Empath

It all started with a book.

Fiction of course, as that's the type of book I have always read for entertainment. Paranormal romance is my favourite genre and if it includes witches or vampires, I will most likely read it.

It was Labour Day weekend in September, 2014, and we decided to go camping. I wanted to "rough it" in an effort to spend quality time with my fiancé, Tyler, and my son, Seth. Mind you, our version of roughing it consisted of a tent with an air mattress, bins of food, lots of clothing and bedding, and fixings for smores. You know, First World roughing it!

We selected a quiet campsite in British Columbia with lots of tress, a lake, and luckily for us, NO BUGS. The most pleasant surprise for me was having no cell phone reception. I had wanted an electronics-free weekend, but Tyler refused to turn his cell phone off in case he received a business call, and Seth wasn't excited about the idea either, because as he put it, "I might get bored." I had to hide my smirk when we realized we had **zero** cell reception. I had gotten exactly what I wanted – family time with my boys.

Tyler always drove any long-distance car journey, while I used my iPad, and Seth kept entertained with various electronics. I had been reading a novel on my iPad called *Haunted on Bourbon Street* by Deanna Chase. *This was the book that changed my life.*

The storyline itself is entertaining, but not important to my story. But the main character of the book is an *empath*. I had **never** heard that word before. I have read tons of paranormal books; so many in fact that I thought I should have seen that description before. How odd that I was resonating with this character described as an *empath!* *How could she be so much like me? This is fiction! This makes no sense to me.*

We had a wonderful weekend of camping and did many touristy activities in nearby towns. We toured a real mine at Sullivan Mine with a retired miner. We went for a ride on an old-fashioned steam engine at Fort Steele. I walked along the edge of the lake in the water nearly losing my sandal in some silt, only to have Seth follow behind me and do exactly the same thing. We made smores, played crib, tossed a ball, built a fire, and enjoyed being outdoors together. Seth had an incident of vomiting during a play the campground put on, and he had to escape fast before he could act out his part, but thankfully he felt better after. All the while, as everything unfolded on our trip, the word *empath* stuck in the back of my mind like an echo haunting me, teasing me.

We drove home on Monday, at our leisure. We stopped in at Turtle Mountain Franks Slide and did the tour, which was utterly depressing. I read a few of the survivors' stories and could not prevent the tears, so I avoided making eye contact with the other tourists. There was a mini movie playing so Tyler, Seth, and I watched it. Seth and I had tears running down our faces at the end. I jokingly asked if he had got dust in his eyes too, which earned me a smile. It was not a place to go for a 'feel good happy go lucky time' that's for sure. I was disturbed to see people wandering over the rocks from the slide where the people of the town were buried. I told Tyler and Seth we would NOT be doing that as it felt disrespectful and creepy.

Back on the road again, Seth plugged his ears in as soon as possible and tuned out everything but his movie. I grabbed my iPad when we had service again. I HAD to look up that word *EMPATH*.

Internet Search: Empath

There were so many hits! So much information on this one word I had never heard before.

"30 traits of an empath (How to know if you are an empath)" published by the Mind Unleashed on October 24, 2013 by Chistel Broederlow.

On my first read, it appeared I had 25 of the 30 traits listed.

"Tyler! Check this out," I exclaimed.

I read it to him and he agreed that yes, I had those traits.

There were lots of quizzes, so I filled out quiz after quiz and they all said the same thing "You are an empath." *How can this be? Empaths are only fictional characters, aren't they?*

I felt so confused.

I continued reading and sharing my findings with Tyler. The descriptions explained so much about me.

You see, I had always thought of myself as an atheist. I never believed in god, religion, or anything. I was skeptical of anything and everything I could not see with my own eyes. The things I could not explain or that could not be explained by science, okay sure, MAYBE there was a higher power. It didn't matter to me either way. I wasn't going to concern myself about the possibilities. I was convinced that when you die that is it. You were done, no more, dust to dust, and food for the bugs.

I had very little experience with death or the loss of loved ones. I barely knew my grandparents and great grandparents on my mother's side, so when they passed on I felt very little loss. I had not attended a funeral until I was an adult, and even then it was an acquaintance from work. The sadness at the funeral felt unbearable more because I mourned for the living, not the lost.

Religion to me seemed like the cause of so much fighting and wars. I saw people claiming religion was behind their actions of judgement and criticism, but it was their right because they were god-fearing folks. The concept of heaven and hell seemed more like a way to control people. As a teenager, I attempted to relate to and understand religion by joining my best friends at their family's church. I also joined the church youth group. I desperately wanted to belong somewhere, and to be a part of a community. I yearned to fit in and be a part of something bigger than me. And above all, I desired to be surrounded by love. While I found most of that, I also found judgement, ego, and unhappiness. If you didn't fit into a specific category then you were flat out wrong. If you divorced you were wrong. It was so black and white with no shades of grey. It didn't feel right for me, so I began to forge my own path. I knew I could be ethical, loving, and accepting of others without god or religion. I decided to follow my instincts and trust myself instead. I was a firm believer that religion had a purpose, and I knew it helped a lot of people, but for some reason, it wasn't right for me.

So as I sat in the car learning about empaths, it felt right, but it also meant believing in something bigger than myself. After all this time could I do that? I was 36 years old at this point and I thought I knew myself. I thought I had established my beliefs or lack of, so why did my being an empath sound and feel so right? I've never had a sense of belonging in this world. I always felt different than other people my age, especially as a child, but I could never explain why. To finally learn there was an explanation which meant I wasn't crazy was a big relief.

My first thought when 'I knew' I was an empath was, *Great! Now how do I get rid of it? I don't want to be like this anymore.* That was September 1, 2014.

Before I go any further I should explain what an empath is. According to Tyler J Hebert; "An empath is a person that is hypersensitive to the emotions and energy of other people, as well as animals. They have the ability to physically feel the emotions of a person/animal standing within their auric field."

No one can say without a doubt exactly what makes a person an Empath. I provided a quiz at the beginning to help you determine if you are or not, based on what I know about most empaths but one thing I have learned is that not all empaths are exactly alike. Here are a list of my empath traits based on what I learned that day:

o **Crowds overwhelm you**
You start out your day feeling great! You want to go to the mall and do a little shopping or go to a concert, maybe you thought you would go to the fair. Yet not even 10 minutes after being in a large group of people you start to get tired, irritable and achy. You're totally miserable and you just want to go home.

o **Moodiness**
Your moods change so quickly, often for what seems like no reason at all. You grasp to find a reason and blame whatever comes to mind. It feels like you are on an emotional roller coaster and you just want off.

o **Pensive/Dreamy**
This will happen most often if the person you are listening to has a monotone voice. With no inflections in their voice you drift away. You may have had difficulty in school because you couldn't stay focused during lectures. You get lost in your thoughts.

o **Stranger's approach you**
Strangers will walk up to you and start telling you very personal things about themselves and their lives. People on the bus will sit beside you and share things you didn't ask about. People on the street feel safe asking you for the time, directions or for help.

o **Unable to watch or read the news**
You find it unbearable to watch the news because of the sad stories. If you overhear it by accident, it upsets you the entire day. You can't read the news because the images of violence and pain disturb you deeply. You skip to the comics and ignore the rest.

o **Violence is agonizing**
You are unable to watch violence on TV or in the movies. Horror movies are just not an option. You feel traumatized every time you hear or see anything related to abuse or cruelty.

o **Awareness of others emotions**
You know how others feel (often better than they do themselves but I highly suggest you never point this out). You sense the underlying emotions of people and animals even if they attempt to hide it.

o **Knowing that someone is lying**
You can usually tell when someone is lying on purpose. You get a bad "feeling" about what they are saying or you can sense that their emotions don't match their words or actions.

o **Low Energy**
You will experience bouts of fatigue for what appears to be no reason. You are in good health, yet you tire easily. You may go through periods of depression.

o **Clutter and disorder affects your energy**
You quickly learn that a messy, untidy space affects your energy. When everything is clean and organized you automatically have more energy and the atmosphere just feels healthier.

o **Attracted to jobs that involve healing or entertainment**
This is not true for everyone but I've found many Empaths seem to be drawn to healing type work like spiritual healers, nurses, doctors, medics, counselors etc. I've also noticed that many gravitate towards the entertainment industry such as acting, musicians, artists, writers etc.

o **Sense energy in food**
Most commonly experienced with meat, an Empath can sometimes sense how the animal died and the trauma of it literally leaves a bad taste in their mouth. They can actually taste the fear of the animal. This causes many to become vegetarians or vegans. For other foods it may be how the foods were treated during processing.

o **Experience others physical symptoms**
Some Empaths can take on the physical symptoms of others such as headaches for example. I find this most commonly happens with loved ones or anyone close to the Empath.

o **Highly sensitive skin**
Those little tags sewn into your clothes drive you insane! Certain fabric hurt your skin because they are too rough. Common household chemicals like scented soaps and dryer sheets cause reactions on your skin.

o **Watches die a slow death**
You've given up on wearing a watch because they never keep the right time or they slowly but surely die not matter how many times you replace the batteries and the watch.

There may be many more traits of an Empath, nevertheless these are the ones that I can identify with and if you can too, then chances are you are an Empath.

I'm not one to ignore the facts when they are staring me in the face but this was a lot to wrap my head around. After a night of sleeping on it, I realized I had been this way my whole life. I'd simply gotten used to being 'different' and as I got older (past those difficult teenage years), I was even proud to be different.

My first thought was, *How can I get rid of this ability?* Yet the next day I came to realize that giving up all these traits or abilities would be the same as walking around completely blind and defenceless, because for me that's exactly what it would feel like. I would no longer know when people were lying to me. I may not have known it at the time but I had relied on these gifts since I was born. They were a part of me, in the same way my limbs are a part of me. These gifts had protected me, and saved me from untold pain, which when I think back makes me *shudder* at the possibilities.

So once I reached that conclusion I knew I needed to learn what it meant to be an empath. Thank goodness for the internet! Everything

I wanted to know was right at my fingertips. One article led to another and then another. Each topic generated more questions and another word to look up. I soon learned there was more than one type of empath. It seemed I was an 'Emotional Empath.' I also discovered that empaths are natural healers, which means an emotional empath can heal others emotionally. You cannot learn to be an empath; you're born that way. I verified that I am a healer by the vertical lines underneath both my pinky fingers, as the palmistry website I came across explained. It was stated that this may be hereditary, so out of curiosity I checked Tyler's hands. He had no vertical lines. Then I checked my mom's hands and she had vertical lines like mine.

I researched palmistry some more but I found it very complicated and soon got bored with it. Shortly after I found a closed groups on Facebook for empaths so I immediately requested to be added to the group but it took three days. At first I read the comments and posts. Most were positive, supportive, and helpful. It was especially helpful to know there were others out there like me. One of the first suggestions I got when I finally posted a comment was to get some crystals for 'grounding' and 'protection.' I asked where I could buy such items, and I was told any metaphysical store. So I returned to the internet search and I found there were two metaphysical stores in Calgary.

Who knew?

Not me, apparently.

CHAPTER 2

Ascension and Crystals

That same day, I went to a metaphysical store in Calgary. The store smelled nice, was decorated in pretty colours, and it seemed comforting. However, the products were unfamiliar to me. I wandered around touching and picking up things, until finally I admitted I had no idea what I was looking for and I asked the sales clerk for some suggestions. I explained I had only found out I was an empath two weeks ago and I felt lost. By the time I left the store I had four black tourmaline crystals for protection, which I was told to put at the four corners of my bed to protect me while I slept. I had white sage to burn around the house to clear negative energy, and I had a book. The total cost was under $30. I picked up the book "Heal Your Body" by Louise Hay that I had bought and I flipped through it a few times, then I read the first chapter, then I skim-read it, but none of it made sense to me, so I put it aside and later lent it to a friend.

I put the stones at the corners of my bed as I was told. I also remembered I had five pink Rose Quartz crystals and I placed them with the black Tourmaline crystals. Then when my mom went to bed I lit the sage. The windows were open so the negative energy could flow out. I felt silly but I walked in a clockwise manner as described and said my intentions under my breath. I wanted the negative energy OUT, to make room for only positive energy. I kept repeating this until I heard my mom say from upstairs, "Do you smell something burning?"

"Yes," I said rather sheepishly. "I'm burning sage." I fully expected the next question to be why? However, to my surprise she said, "Okay" and then there was silence once more. I figured she was used to my weirdness.

I cleared the main floor and the upstairs, getting in each nook and cranny as best as I could. The smoke bothered my throat a little and the smell reminded me of burning marijuana, but I didn't let that deter me. I opened a window or door on each floor to let the negative energy flow out. My fiancé sat quietly on the couch not at all bothered by my activity. When my rabbit smelled the smoke she became a little distressed by it. To her I'm sure it meant danger and she thumped on the floor a few times to let us know she was agitated.

That night I slept like a log! I had not slept that well in ages. Ever since my son was born I've struggled with insomnia or waking during the night. I've also suffered from night terrors, even as an adult. I get nightmares like everyone else, but actual night terrors are different. I've read that only kids have them and they grow out them. I've always been a night owl too, so I never seem to fall asleep at a decent time. I don't know if it was the sage or the stones/crystals nor did I care. I was so grateful to feel rested the next day, I knew I had to get more crystals and I was more than willing to try some other new things.

Someone on Facebook told me some people can feel the energy in crystals. That each crystal has its own 'vibration' that can be used to aid in healing, and many other things. I had to try it so I held some crystals, but I felt nothing. I was a little disappointed. I purchased the ones that caught my eye. I loved the multitude of colours and shapes. I felt like I was choosing and holding treasure. It might seem silly but having these crystals made me smile and that was enough.

After about a week I suddenly noticed a couple of my crystals made a tingling sensation in my hand, almost like electricity but not as strong or violent. In a matter of days I could feel that same tingling in all of my crystals except the ones that were for grounding energy.

With those I didn't feel anything at all. Somehow I managed to tune into their frequency, but I don't know how.

Since I learnt that I was an empath, within days I started experiencing odd symptoms and signs, which seemed unexplainable. Every question I had could be confirmed or rejected within minutes of looking it up on the internet. I would check and re-check multiple sources to confirm the information was accurate. So when I started having these 'symptoms,' including tingling, blurred vision, seeing colours that would quickly disappear, chills, extreme fatigue, aches and pains, I learned it was all normal for someone going through an ascension or spiritual awakening. Thank goodness, as I thought I might have the flu or something.

By the way, ascension, if you didn't already know, means increasing your vibration to keep up with the changing vibration of the Universe.

For me, the ascension process felt long and drawn out. The fatigue was the hardest to cope with as I would wake up tired and take naps during the afternoons on weekends. After work during the week I'd lie on the couch and fall asleep for an hour or more then go up to bed and fall right back to sleep. My son would sit near me and quietly play his handheld games. I kept wondering if I was truly sick or if this was all normal symptoms of a spiritual awakening? I had not felt this tired since my pregnancy with Seth and the first year after he was born.

One piece of advice I seemed to be seeing and hearing repeatedly was to trust myself and not to question every feeling and thought. If my gut feeling was strong, I never questioned it. Yet for everything else, I had to apply reasoning to every motive or action. If I liked something, such as a particular crystal, for example, then why did I like it? Was I meant to have it? Was it important? When I was selecting crystals and attracted to a certain colour I would ask myself, *Do I only like the colour or is this a crystal I need?* Was I being directed to it? What if it was the wrong one?

ARGH!

I was driving myself crazy. I told myself, *Who cares?! Stop over-analyzing every little thing!* That's what the advice means when someone says, "Listen to your heart not your head." It comes down to, does it *feel* right for me? If the answer is yes then go with it. You don't have to know 'why' for everything. I had to stop trying to control every little thing. Nowadays, if my first thought is positive it's good, and if my first thought or feeling is wariness I trust that. In the past, as soon as I started questioning myself, I would talk myself out of what I already knew was right. If you can't trust yourself, then who can you trust?

CHAPTER 3

Spirit Guides

As I was coming to terms with all of this I read a little about spirit guides. Someone had mentioned it in a blog and the words caught my attention. I had no idea if I had one but I suspected so, and I realized they may have saved my butt a few times as a kid! I wanted to know for sure if I had one. I read the theories about what spirit guides were and what they did, but it all meant little to me. At times I felt like I was learning a new language and new words. I thought I had a fairly extensive vocabulary but every day I had to look up a new term to see what it meant.

That week, a kind woman on Facebook offered to do a free card reading for me. I wasn't about to refuse when I had so many questions and seemingly no direction. She laid out the cards and took a picture and sent it to me. To me it looked like nothing more than a bunch of cards.

Then she sent me her interpretation. She said she saw two of my spirit guides. One was a very protective man, and the other was either a dog or a wolf, black or brown-coloured. The rest of the message was lost on me, but what she said about the spirit guides stuck with me.

The next day I went to pick Seth up from his day-home, as I did every weekday after work. While waiting for him to gather his things I glanced at the hallway lamp in the entryway and asked his caregiver,

Rhonda (yes this is her real name), why the lamp was never on. She explained it was a salt rock lamp given to her by her mother and it was for dispelling negative energy. I laughed and said, "It won't work very well if it's never on."

As I said this, I realized Rhonda knows about spiritual stuff and had for quite some time. I wasn't interested in it before so I never paid much attention and felt we probably didn't have much in common. Seth adored Rhonda and her children, and he cried when it was home time because he wanted to stay and play longer. So I knew it was the right place for my son and I had overlooked any differences Rhonda and I had in child rearing or lifestyle. This lamp gave me the courage to start talking to her about what I had been experiencing lately, and she opened right up to me. I mentioned the card reading and she agreed that she too had noticed a male presence over my right shoulder, and that he seemed very protective. That gave me the confirmation I needed to know that I did, in fact, have spirit guides!

I wanted my own set of cards, so I could communicate with my guides. I asked the person on Facebook if I could buy the cards and would they work for me? I was told absolutely, and to buy whatever cards caught my eye.

I returned to the store and checked out every single box, but I didn't like any apart from the deck with the wolf on the front. I loved wolves and owls. The store had a sample box, so I looked at the cards inside and I loved the artwork, too. The bad news was, the store was out of stock and they would not sell me the sample box. So I walked around again looking at the other options while pouting. I couldn't see any others I liked so I drove all the way across the city in rush hour traffic to go to the only other metaphysical store I knew of, to see if they had the same cards with the wolf and owl on the front of the box. They did, so I snatched them up fast, and I also purchased a few more crystals.

That evening we were heading out camping with friends. During the car ride to the campsite I held my newfound treasures in my lap. I was holding my new Selenite crystal and the darn thing zapped me, sharp enough that I dropped it. *What the heck was that about?*

The next morning while Tyler slept, I rose early, opened my new cards, and read the instructions. I had to cleanse each card and attune them to my energy before I could use them. I am not the most patient person so this didn't thrill me. I reluctantly followed the cleansing instructions. I had to burn sage and hold the card in the smoke so both sides were immersed in it, while stating my intentions. The sage wouldn't stay lit and it took forever.

But finally I could give myself a reading!

I chose to draw three cards, one for past, one for present and one for future. And that's when I learned my spirit guides had a sense of humour.

Present day card: 'A New Day Dawns. Today is a new day...Enjoy the day.'

I laughed out loud "Very funny, you smart asses!" Actually it was pretty funny because it was quite early in the morning and we were out camping after all. The past and future cards were more serious and seemed fitting. I knew the reading was accurate and I suppose this was their way of proving it.

When Tyler awoke he asked what I was doing, and I told him. Then I offered to do a card reading for him. I warned him that I had no clue if it would work on other people. It felt like it did work though. Then I offered to do one for my friend, Sandra, but I had a little more trouble doing hers. The next night I tried to do one for my son and his dad but I felt frustrated because it felt like I was forcing it.

I kept Tyler apprised of most of my A-HA moments, and he was outwardly supportive, but I knew he was skeptical. Some of it he accepted willingly, and the rest he either disregarded or kept his opinion to himself. No matter, I appreciated him all the more for it. I've always felt his love for me, but this was a true test of his tolerance and willingness to love me no matter what. I knew if I truly was a healer, I wanted to use it to help him in any way I could.

Three weeks after learning I was an empath I was introduced to a woman at work named Colleen (this is her real name) who sat around the corner from me. As we chatted about work-related topics I noticed her necklace, which had a Moonstone and an Amethyst (my birthstone). I complimented her on it and we chatted about where she got it.

Out of the blue Colleen said. "You need to get a Yellow Citrine crystal." I must have looked skeptical because she apologized and said sometimes things like that pop into her head. I said I would get one as soon as I could, although neither of us knew what it was for. That week I went back to the metaphysical store and bought a Yellow Citrine crystal, as well as a Moonstone crystal because I liked it so much. The Yellow Citrine didn't vibrate for me so I thought maybe I had got a dud. The next time I saw her at work I showed it to her. She held it and said it was a very grounding stone. "How do you know?" I asked. She explained that, "It felt like a heavy weight bringing her down to earth." Then she had to go so I couldn't ask her any further questions. I knew meeting her was no accident. Clearly she knew a lot about this stuff, and she was easily accessible. I spent a day drumming up the courage to ask her to join me for lunch, which she readily accepted.

Over lunch we made small talk while I worked up the nerve to ask her how she knew so much about the crystals. Finally I asked and she smiled knowingly. She gave me some of her background and went on to explain that she was a messenger for the other side. I knew she wasn't lying. She went on to describe my spirit guides to me. There was a man over my right shoulder whose appearance seemed organic and he wore a checkered shirt. There was a dog or something that was mostly black with brown on my right, and an older woman with white hair and a large bosom on my left. The woman represented feminism and was not always there, but she came and went. Colleen asked me if that seemed right but I didn't know. Since I had lost very few people in my life, none of them seemed to match those who had passed on.

She went on to say my guides had a message for me. The oracle cards I was learning to use were meant for me and me alone right now. That's why they weren't working well when I tried to give others a reading. They used the example that it was like learning to dance and trying to teach others the steps at the same time. I could understand that, sort of, but it felt a little like I had had my hand slapped. I had meant well as I wanted to help my friends and family. I agreed I wouldn't do anymore card readings, but that didn't stop me from sulking.

I continued to use my cards every chance I got. I was so excited about having spirit guides even if I could not see them. I assumed they could hear me if I addressed them out loud. I didn't know for sure but talking out loud to them felt right. Whenever I used the cards I mostly got the same ones repeatedly, maybe as reminders to keep the ideas at the forefront of my mind. The consistency helped cement into my mind that the messages were real and I should heed them. The messages seemed vague at times, or more likely, I didn't understand them. Other messages I did understand but didn't necessarily want to hear. Several of the messages gave me hope and peace.

CHAPTER 4

Chakras

Learning about chakras has been an eye-opening experience to say the least. I had heard the term before and I remember people referring to the third eye but that ended the extent of my knowledge on the subject. I looked up the term Chakra:

("chakra." YourDictionary)
chak·ra
in certain forms of yoga, traditional Asian medicine, etc., any of a number of points in the human body, usually seven, that are considered centers of physical or spiritual energy: see chi

The information I initially gleaned was that chakras made up seven primary points within the body, but they were not vital organs. The concept was that energy should flow from the crown (top of the head) through each chakra in a straight line down the body to the root chakra (base of the tailbone) and into the earth. I purchased a book called *The Complete Guide to Chakras* by Ambika Wauters. The book has a simple layout, with pictures and simple explanations. For now I use the book as a reference guide only, and I have yet to read it cover to cover. What I did learn, however, was that chakras can be blocked, closed, or gunked up, and when that happens it can affect your physical and mental health.

Clearing chakras can be done through meditation or Reiki. Since there seemed to be a YouTube video for everything I started my research and learning there. There were plenty of guided instructional videos I could try to clear my own chakras if they needed it.

Well, that felt like a colossal failure, as for one thing, you have to be able to meditate.

Meditation is probably the single most frustrating thing I have tried to do in my life! Everyone says, "You need to meditate," "Meditation is key," "Meditation solves all your problems," and so on.

First, I had to learn how to sit still without doing something, let alone trying to empty my mind!

So far, attempts: 8; Success: 0.

As soon as I sat down to meditate, something would itch, twitch or scratch!

If I got past that, by changing clothes, rearranging the blankets, changing positions ten times, and finally attempting to try to empty my mind, then I would suddenly remember ALL the things I had forgotten to do that day. So I would go off to do these things, convinced I wouldn't be able to properly relax until I had. And by then it would be bedtime! Meditation is clearly a work in progress for me. I guess my chakras will have to stay blocked for now. Assuming they are blocked at all.

So that leaves Reiki as the only other option I am aware of, for clearing my chakras or finding out if they are blocked or closed.

"What is Reiki?" Search.

("reiki." YourDictionary)
Rei·ki
an alternative healing technique thought by some to reduce stress, pain, etc. through the transfer of a certain kind of energy from the hands of a practitioner to parts of the body of a person suffering from such symptoms

Totally not what I thought it was at all. Healing through energy, huh? Yet the more I read about it the quicker I realized I'd done this before. I recall when my ex-husband and I were first dating he had a terrible sinus headache and was totally stuffed up. He was so miserable and I felt awful for him, so I offered to relieve the pressure for him. He figured it couldn't hurt and he laid down with his head in my lap. I'm not sure exactly what I did other than repeatedly running my fingertips down from the top of his sinuses along his nose and along the sides of his ears to his throat for quite some time until all of a sudden he exclaimed that his sinuses had suddenly drained and he could breathe. The pressure was gone and his headache eased.

So now I wondered if I had been healing people emotionally and physically all my life. I must have natural abilities I never questioned because I thought everyone could do it.

To be sure, as soon as Tyler complained about having a headache again I offered to try and take the pain away. I had him lay back on the couch with his head on my lap and I rubbed and pressed wherever seemed to make sense with a little mint oil on my hands. He whined that I used too much of the oil, making his eyes water, but after a short time his headache had gone. I knew if there was a physical underlying cause it would come back, and sure enough the next day he had a full blown headache again. So I made him drink water, eat a healthy meal, and take some vitamins, then I took his headache away, again. After that it didn't return.

Since I have not been attuned to Reiki, I feel like I have to be touching the person to help but I don't know how to do it properly. It seems I can only take away minor aches and pains for those I love. I haven't tried it on anyone else. For now I'm happy to help my family in small ways. I read that you cannot cause harm with Reiki, which made me feel better.

CHAPTER 5

Astrology and Numerology

It had been ten weeks since I discovered I was an empath. During that time I had learned a great deal about myself; more as each day passed.

For example, I learned some interesting things about my birth sign. I am a Pisces, a water sign of the zodiac and the twelfth and final sign in the zodiacal cycle. This sign is known to bring together the characteristics of the eleven signs before it. Feelings define the Pisces and their intuition is highly evolved.

Pisces traits (traditional):

-   Imaginative and sensitive
-   Compassionate and kind
-   Selfless and unworldly
-   Intuitive and sympathetic.

These are all traits of the average empath, if empaths could be considered average.

There is plenty of information out there for each zodiac sign so I won't go into a lot of detail but for me it was another piece of the puzzle that clicked neatly into place.

When I finally lost interest in reading about my horoscope sign I went from Astrology to Numerology. I found multiple numerology explanations in books and websites that explained how do figure out my own life path number, expression, and soul urge. Mine are as follows:

'Life Path' is 9
The life path number is supposed to be the most important number.

'Expression' is 3
Also known as the destiny number.

'Soul Urge' is 4
Refers to as the heart's desire.

When I read the descriptions for each they seemed to describe me very well but in a general way. Each site seemed to have a slightly different version but most of it applied. Not everything applied 100 percent because we are all individual with different upbringings, cultures, and mindsets. Still, it was fun and interesting to see myself described objectively. It told me that I had been born an empath and not everything about my personality was because of how I was raised. Not everything about me was a learned trait. Instead, it appeared that who I am, and who I have always been, was already ingrained in my DNA. So no one, not my biological parents, nor anyone else who helped to raise me could take credit for ALL that I am.

CHAPTER 6

$\blacklozenge$ ━━━━━━ ✦ ━━━━━━ $\blacklozenge$

Old Soul

I have always known I was born old. When I was young I took on the responsibilities of my younger brothers, Damon who is three years younger, and Colin who is four years younger. I would insist on changing Damon's diapers, dressing him, and mothering him.

It was easy for me to talk to adults and understand them, so it annoyed me when they spoke to me like a child, even though I was one.

As a teenager, I defied all authority that I did not agree with. I wasn't a troublemaker by any means. But was I difficult? Oh yes. Very.

I was drawn to friends who were not on the path of upstanding citizens yet when they smoked or did drugs, I had no interest. I tried smoking, but it hurt my lungs so I didn't see the point of it. I was more curious than anything about what they were doing and trying to understand why they did it. They always offered and I always said "*no, thank you*". I never felt peer pressure but instead I got the comment, "That's smart of you."

I didn't judge them, as they seemed to have their reasons for what they did, or they thought they did anyway. I found it odd that they knew they were doing something that was not in their best interests, yet they seemed desperate not to be different from their peers.

I also hung out with the "cool kids" during school, but after school hours I seemed to always find myself with the troubled kids and I didn't fit in with either group. I was more like an outsider looking in, fascinated by their antics and sometimes I tried to guide them on a better path, but I didn't always succeed. At times it was like my advice fell on deaf ears.

I was never one to fold to peer pressure and I had a very strong attitude about what I believed was right and wrong. Some things I could let slide but not violence on animals or people. I would not stand for bullying, even if my sticking up for the underdog made me a target. I would never agree to anything that put someone else in danger or jeopardy.

It was not uncommon for me to give advice to people older than I. They would say how smart I was, how I was so much older than my age, so mature, but it seemed like the advice I gave was rarely taken onboard. I knew when adults were making poor decisions. Sadly, as a child I did not have control of most situations so I frequently suffered at the hands of their bad choices and lack of good judgement. So when I say I defied authority, what I mean is I only respected those who respected me in turn. If you treated me as a human being with rights and opinions, I would do the same in return. If you tried to force your opinions on me and take away my power and freedom, woe is you.

Those who raised me suffered a great deal of stress due to their inability to manage me appropriately. When I was grounded for what I deemed a ridiculous reason, I would sneak out and wander the streets in the middle of the night until the police would pick me up and take me home asking my guardians, "Is she yours? We found her wandering the streets."

Even with incidents such as these, I was always known by family and friends as the reliable, dependable one. If I said I would do something then I would do it, barring unforeseen circumstances of course. I lived a very transient life so friends would come and go. New schools brought more of the same challenges of not fitting into any group. When I did make friends they were almost always much older than me because it was the only way I could relate to anyone.

Still, what seemed like common sense to me clearly did not to everyone. When you are young, being different or odd in any way can be quite distressing, especially since I was the sociable sort. I may not have needed to fit in, but I did want to have friends. I wanted to belong to a group or community because I would often get lonely. I was okay with being mature for my age because I had always been that way so I accepted that as a part of my personality. I never seemed to have any difficulties attracting a boyfriend either, but more often than not they would use me in some way or I would sense they were troubled and want to help. That was not a good start to a healthy relationship. I had even more difficulty making friends with girls, so my options were few.

Another piece of the puzzle snapped into its rightful place when I found out that I most certainly am an old soul.

The soul starts out as a young soul and has as many lives as required to learn certain "lessons" before they move on to the next stage, which is like a teenage soul and so on. These "lessons" can only be learned on the physical plane. From what I understand we were all created at the same time but we don't all learn our "lessons" at the same rate. We also have a choice as to when we reincarnate, which might be a few years after the last time we were here, or many years later. So it matters not where we are in our stages. It's neither better nor worse. We are not in competition with each other; it's simply the path our souls follow. With this information I learnt that yes, I am an old soul and I used my pendulum to confirm it (I will explain about the pendulum in the next chapter).

The reason why understanding this meant so much to me, was that it gave me the confirmation I needed about WHY I was so different from other people all my life. Besides being an empath, I was also very old!

I'd never believed in life after death before and now I was learning that we reincarnate many times! It seems the more I learn; the less I know. So that makes me wonder, how many times did I have to reincarnate to reach the stage I'm at now? How much time is there in between each reincarnation? How old am I really in Earth years? Maybe I don't want to know, but hey, I look good for my age!

CHAPTER 7

Pendulum

On one of my many trips to the metaphysical store these lovely pendulums caught my eye. At first I just admired them but I had no clue what they were for. Still I knew I would love to have one. My following trip to the store is when I finally learned about them.

A clerk I had not met before was working and she was eager to answer questions and share her experiences with me, which I greatly appreciated. She explained how to use a pendulum. I was told to rinse it under water to clear its energy first so the pendulum could absorb my energy and attune to me. She went on to tell me that it could only answer yes or no questions. To attune it to me I had to hold it up and still, and ask simple questions I already knew the answers to, such as, "Do I have a son?" Obviously I do, so it should say yes. I should clarify that yes is forward and back and no is side to side. Then I needed to ask it a question I knew had an answer of no, and I had to check it swung from side to side.

It seemed simple enough, so I selected a pendulum I liked the colour of, which was only $5.

When I got it home, after holding it for some time, I held the end with the smaller crystals, dangling the larger crystal about 2cm off the table, and using my left hand to stabilize my right arm. I did not want to get any false readings because that would totally defeat the purpose. Besides, I wanted to know if it really worked as I'd never seen one in action before. I asked, "Am I a girl?" It was slow at first but I received an answer the first time! I was so freaking excited! It was magic! After a few more questions, I knew it was working.

I didn't understand how this was possible, so I did some digging on the internet and came back with the answer that it works off your own vibrations from your own subconscious.

I liked asking it questions anyway so I carried on and soon discovered that it would not or could not answer questions about other people. So I tried asking some spiritual questions about myself. Those were ignored as the pendulum did not budge at all. I asked it a few more questions and some were answered with the pendulum turning in a complete circle, which I took to mean unsure. So technically it had four answers: yes, no, unsure, and not answering that question.

The best was when I asked about my spirit guides.

Question: "Do I have more than three spirit guides?"
Answer: No.

Question: "Do I have exactly three spirit guides?"
Answer: Yes.

Question: "Is one of my spirit guides a dog?"
Answer: No.

Question: "Is one of my spirit guides a wolf?"
Answer: Yes

Question: "Is my spirit guide a male?"
Answer: HUGE Swing for "NO," which made me laugh out loud.

Question: "Is my spirit guide a female?"
Answer: Gentle swing for "Yes"

Somehow I think my pendulum was influenced by certain 'guides' with those last two answers. So I have a female wolf spirit guide? That's pretty cool. I've always loved wolves.

I quickly learned that there is a limit to how many questions you can ask in one sitting before it stops answering all together.

The next day I got my mom involved and I told her to ask me something from my childhood that I would not remember. She mentioned a few things but I remembered them. Finally she thought of something I couldn't remember fully.

Question: "Did my cousin try to feed me poisonous mushrooms intentionally?"
Answer: Yes

"That little brat! I'm so glad I tattled on him back then."

My mom exclaimed, "I knew it! We always suspected, but never knew for sure."

So when the information came up about the old soul and I wanted to know where I was on that chart, I grabbed my pendulum again.

Question: "Am I an old soul?"
Answer: Yes.

Question: "Have I incarnated more than 500 times?"
Answer Yes.

Question: "Have I incarnated more than 700 times?"
Answer: Yes.

I think I'll stop there for now.

I've always considered myself a rational individual, so for me to so quickly accept and trust this pendulum signalled a big change in my beliefs. Still, I KNEW I wasn't making that pendulum move with my hand on purpose because I really wanted honest answers. Besides, I wasn't trying to convince anyone but myself, and I trust myself.

Now I knew I had a wolf spirit guide I looked up totem wolf meanings, which are: Loyalty, Cunning, Generosity, Intelligence, Friendliness, Compassionate, and Communication. The Wolf Totem also happened to be my birth animal for the month and date I was born.

I later learned there was another use for pendulums. You can clear crystals using a pendulum simply by holding the pendulum above a crystal. The pendulum will automatically start spinning in circles above the crystal in a clockwise motion, and then once the crystal is cleared it will spin in a counter-clockwise motion to charge the crystal, and when it's done it will stop on its own.

CHAPTER 8

Grounding

Grounding, as I have learned, is very important for people like me, and I don't mean like, "Stay in the house, you're grounded."

I like to think of it as more like an electrical current. The science behind it is that all the energy wants to go back into the ground, which is why we ground through our feet. The earth grounds us. We know we are a source of electricity, and also conductors. So as I learned with chakras, the energy enters in through our head, down through seven points in our bodies, and out into the ground or earth. So if you wear rubber-soled shoes, leather, or glass slippers then your body will have difficulty grounding because rubber, leather, and glass cannot conduct electricity. That's why cars are the safest place to be if you are near a downed power pole because the rubber on the tires will protect you.

So what happens when you are not grounded properly?

I could never understand why my moods changed so quickly. At times I thought I might be bi-polar. I would suddenly get so irritated even when there seemed to be no source for it. I could easily over-react or wake up moody. I would try to find any reason which would explain my low mood, even if that meant blaming the nearest person. I would go into a shopping mall and 20 minutes later I would be miserable, achy, and grouchy, and I wanted to go home right away. I would quickly snap at whoever I was with.

I think I finally understand why. I wasn't menstrual, I wasn't bi-polar. I was an emotional empath. An emotional empath takes on the emotions of others, both good and bad. An emotional empath absorbs the emotional energies of those around them as if the emotions are their own. If you're grounded, you're not affected quite as bad, but you're still affected. Guess what happens when you're in a mall with a crowd of people and your shoes have rubber soles? The energy gets trapped.

I found gardening helped to calm me down. It was very relaxing and a solitary activity for me. In winter I struggled with depression and tried to book vacations near the ocean. It's no wonder those activities helped. With gardening you are touching and working with the earth. When you are at the beach you walk barefoot. All the energies which did not belong to me would drain away when my bare skin touched the earth. The added bonus is that salt water also cleanses your "aura" of negative energy so swimming in the ocean helped me to restore some semblance of an emotionally stable individual. In case you've never heard the term aura before, here is the definition:

("aura." YourDictionary)

au·ra

noun

1. an invisible emanation or vapor, as the aroma of flowers
2. a particular atmosphere or quality that seems to arise from and surround a person or thing: enveloped in an *aura* of grandeur
3. a field of energy thought by some to emanate from all things in nature and to be visible to certain persons with psychic powers

I could never figure out why I seemed to be stressed out and right back to how I felt before my vacations, only a week or so after returning home. What's funny is that I have never liked socks. My preference all summer would be to walk barefoot everywhere, but of course that would not be sanitary or safe. So my second choice is flip flops, and when I am in my own back yard I kick them off and walk barefoot. Little did I know that I was grounding myself.

I noticed that exercise helped as well, especially when I jogged outdoors alongside a river or near trees. Nature is a huge factor for healing empaths.

It's not really an option to never wear shoes, and most, if not all footwear has rubber soles, so crystals were the answer. Certain crystals have grounding properties. Remember I said my co-worker Colleen told me to get a Yellow Citrine crystal, which was very grounding? That's why I needed it. There are other crystals that also help with grounding, such as Fire Agate. I purchased a book called *The Crystal Bible* by Judy Hall that features over 200 crystals. It's a fantastic reference book that I use frequently now.

I remember a day when I could have really used my grounding crystals. My son had his tenth birthday party and we were all over at his dad's place. Seth had nine friends over for his party. We had planned activities and cake, of course. Things were great, the kids were playing, and I had taken some photos. The kids were very loud so we were glad all us adults could all be upstairs while the kids were all downstairs. The kids were like little molecules bouncing off each other! Half an hour into the party I started to feel a headache coming on. An hour in and it felt like a migraine and I had to lie down on the couch. I was so tired I fell asleep! I was woken up when it was time to do the cake and open presents, but my head still hurt. I rarely get headaches and it was even rarer to get one for no apparent reason.

Then I remembered I had left all my crystals at home. After we left the party I felt better, but once I got home I held my Yellow Citrine right away and it helped. So even happy, excitable energy can bombard an empath, not only negative energy.

Another time I could have used grounding was when I was at work. A co-worker asked to talk to me about a personal matter. We would go into a private room and talk. She got a little teary as she talked and the emotions came off her in waves, so much so that I felt shaky and my stomach went all jittery. Then it occurred to me that I had left my grounding crystal in my purse at my desk. So when I went back to my desk I picked up the grounding crystal and immediately I calmed right down. It completely took me by surprise because I wondered if my blood sugar was low. It turns out I just needed to ground myself better.

Even with the crystals I find I can still get overwhelmed by the end of the day. The crystals cannot take care of everything 100 percent, though they help a lot throughout the day. Still, there are especially stressful days, and when on those days I come straight home, run a bath, and dump a full cup of Epson salts into the bath water. I soak until I feel better. It works every time but it's not an option to have a bath whenever I feel like it.

Since I started carrying my crystals every day and taking salt baths as needed, I have been able to think clearly, stabilize my emotions, and I have even felt HAPPY! Every day is no longer a struggle and some of my aches and pains have even been reduced.

A few people told me that if you picture roots growing out of your feet into the ground that also helps to ground yourself. I've tried it but it doesn't have the same effect on me.

CHAPTER 9

◆———✦———◆

Angel Signs and Numbers

Another topic that I kept reading in blogs was to watch for signs from the Universe, or signs from angels. Now I had a lot of trouble with the concept of angels. It seemed odd since I readily accepted that I had spirit guides, but the idea of angels being real was too farfetched for me. I'm guessing it's because I associated angels with religion, and even with everything I had come to terms with, organized religion was still not one of them. I'm aware religion has its place in society and does plenty of good things, but my mind was made up. I wanted no part of it.

The most common sign to watch for, I learned, was numbers. Numerous people said they would identify repeating numbers like 1111 or 4444, and each set of numbers carries a message. It's all fully explained in Doreen Virtue's book, *Angel Numbers 101*. Since I heard that, I started watching for these signs, only to be sorely disappointed as no repeating numbers came up for me. Whatever! Angels didn't exist anyway so what did I care?

A few days later I was walking to my office building when I saw a massive sign on a building I had been walking past for years. It was a building where they helped the unfortunate, so they had painted the side of the building with hands releasing a dove. They were selling the building so over top of the painted side of the building there was a huge sign saying FOR SALE with a phone number. The last four digits were 1111. *How long has that been there*, I wondered? Probably just a coincidence because I was looking for it. At least that's what I thought until I saw a license plate with the number 1111. Okay, weird. Then another license plate with the number 111.

What's the harm in looking up what the numbers mean? I'm curious.

Internet search: "Angel number 1111"

"The repeating number 1 sequence (in all its forms) is most often the first sequence that appears to many people. Once the 1111 is acknowledged, the number sequence changes to another combination along with new messages, life experiences, directions, and opportunities. Many people associate the repeating 1111 with a wakeup call, a code of activation or code of consciousness/awakening code."

Mind blown.

According to Doreen Virtue's book *Angel Numbers 101*; "*111* this number brings you the urgent message that your thoughts are manifesting instantly, so keep your mind-set focused upon your desires. Give any fearful thoughts to Heaven for transmutation."

A couple days after that the same sign that was on that building had been flipped onto the roof by the wind and stayed there for a few days or a week. The next thing I knew, it had been removed. I didn't see repeating ones again and I was looking, hard.

The next set of repeating numbers didn't happen immediately. I'd almost given up even watching for them anymore. When it did happen I saw 7's on a license plate, 777. Nothing to get too excited about. As I neared my parking lot a bus passed in front of me with the numbers 7777 on the side. I crossed the street and two cars passed in front of me. Both of them had 777 on their license plates. "Okay," I said out loud, "I got the message."

Internet search: "Angel number 777"

"Repeating 7's indicates for you to keep up the great work you've been doing of late. Your angels are telling you that you are on the right path and you will find that things of a positive nature will flow freely for you."

According to Doreen Virtue's book *Angel Numbers 101*; "*777* you are definitely on the right path in every area of your life. Stay balanced and spiritually aware so that you can continue moving forward on this illuminated path."

When I was picking Seth up that day I was telling Rhonda about these numbers I saw.

"That's great," she said. "Maybe you can ask for something you need."

"What do you mean?" I asked.

"I mean, you can ask the Universe for help when you need it and help will be provided. Just be careful what you ask for," she explained.

"Be careful how?" I asked.

"For me, when my husband was away from town for work, I wanted him to come home. He was supposed to be gone for one full week. He was back in two days. Yes, I wanted him home, but at the same time we really needed the money. So like I said, be careful what you ask for," Rhonda explained.

The following week I got an email that I would be losing my underground parking spot. There were options for parking outside but they were quite expensive and I was worried about the monthly cost of parking because I was a commuter. I said out loud, "I really need affordable parking please. I simply cannot afford to park in the lot I'm using now and I don't have any other options at the moment. I could really use some help please, and thank you."

The VERY next day as I was driving to my usual parking lot I saw a massive sign showing the cost of parking in a different lot for $3 a day less than my usual lot. So I parked there and said my thank you's. Then two days later the sign came down. I went to pay and discovered parking had gone up by a dollar. As I read the new sign I saw they had monthly parking, which would save me another $44 a month. So

I went online to request a spot and saw I would have to apply and be put on a waiting list. Well drat again. I apply anyhow. Could take a month, could take a year, they don't say but I'll never get it if I didn't try. A few weeks later I received an email that I got a spot and I had three days to take it. Not only did I get 24/7 parking but it was close to the gate I need to go through to get to work.

Did I have help?

I can't say for sure but I did ask and I did get what I asked for...

CHAPTER 10

Reiki Healing

Since I didn't truly believe my weak attempt at meditation and clearing even one chakra worked, I decided to seek out a Master Reiki practitioner. I chose to look for someone in a small town near my cottage where I spent my weekends, since I knew I wouldn't be able to go during the week due to my full-time job. A quick internet search, and a few emails later, I had an appointment booked for the weekend after Thanksgiving, in October 2014. There was a write-up of the practitioner Patty and I liked her photo so I trusted that.

I didn't know what to expect since this was all new to me. I had read that it was important to set the intention of what you wanted to achieve during a session. My intention was to clear my chakras and I made a point of asking my guides to assist me.

I arrived at my appointment on time, which was amazing since I got lost on the way. As soon as I walked in Patty was coming down the hall and she exclaimed, "Wow, your energy is amazing!"

"Thank you," I said, even though I had no clue what she meant.

We went back into her room which was set up the same way a massage therapist would set up their rooms for clients. I laid on the bed/table fully clothed. She offered me a blanket but it was too warm for that. I was comfortable, so I closed my eyes and relaxed. I wasn't overly concerned with what she was doing, which is rather odd for me. Normally I'm curious about everything. Nonetheless, we were chatting while she was moving around me when halfway through I suddenly got VERY dizzy. I felt like I was going to fall off the table yet I was still lying in the same spot!

"Holy smokes!" I exclaimed, "I'm really, really dizzy."

"Well, I'm not surprised" Patty said. "I just removed a weight off your heart chakra the size of a bowling ball!"

After the session I was light headed, so I had to take my time and have a cup of tea. I asked if that happened to everyone.

"Nope, not everyone," Patty explained, "actually every person is totally different so you can't tell people what to expect necessarily because it's based on the individual, their experiences, and what they want from the session. Also, every practitioner is slightly different based on their preferred techniques and their specific gifts. Sometimes you have to go to a couple of different Reiki practitioners before you find the right fit for you personally."

Once the light headedness went away I called Tyler to tell him what had happened. I was feeling really good. Lighter is the best way I can describe it. Once I got home I wanted to go for a nice long walk with Tyler and my mom's dog since it was such a beautiful warm fall day. I NEVER walk anywhere unless I have to, so this was totally not like me. I felt amazing, so energized and animated. I was talking non-stop the entire walk. That was Saturday. Patty had checked in with me to see how I was doing. I was impressed that she took the time to ask, and I let her know how great I felt directly after my first session.

On Sunday I didn't feel quite as amazing but not bad either, just not super-charged anymore. Monday I woke up and went to work but I wasn't feeling so good. I had been drinking a lot of water, which was odd for me since I dislike water and generally prefer herbal tea. I was craving water though, and could not seem to stay hydrated. I wasn't sick but I felt "off." Tuesday started off worse with my stomach bothering me. I went to work but while I was there I felt nauseous and my temperature was spiking. By 1 p.m. I gave up and went home sick. That night I was SO SICK with severe diarrhoea, a headache, dehydration, and exhaustion. I had to take the next two days off work and I slept through most of it. I knew I didn't have the flu and suspected it had something to do with the Reiki.

I checked online and according to one reference, on occasion some people may experience what is known as a healing crisis but it's rare to experience severe symptoms. As the body's seven primary chakras open up and allow the energy to flow, your body will naturally begin to eliminate toxins from environmental, medicinal, emotional, and stress. This is apparently a good thing. I was quite positive that this is what I was experiencing, and since it meant achieving a better state of health I knew I could handle it and it should be temporary.

Two weeks later, I had another Reiki session with Patty. I had been warned it would take more than one session because when your chakras aren't used to being open they will naturally return to the sluggish state of moving energy until fully cleared and your body has a chance to heal fully. That doesn't happen in a day. My second session was quite different than the first one and very personal in nature, so I won't go into a lot of detail but it's important to mention one thing as it comes up again later on. I was asked if I ever had a miscarriage.

"No," I said, "Not that I know about."

"Ok," Patty replied, "I saw a baby girl in the room with us and thought maybe she was here for you but maybe she is here for me." As she said the words I knew it wasn't true. The rest of the session regarded my childhood and the peace of mind I had after that was worth its weight in gold and long overdue.

That evening, as I lay in bed, I could not stop thinking about what had been said. I knew she was fibbing when she said maybe the baby was there for her, but her intention was good. So maybe she didn't think I was ready to hear it? What was she protecting me from?

Right after my marriage to Jacob (Seth's dad) in 2002, we had really wanted a baby. I wanted a boy so badly. Not a girl, but only because of my traumatic childhood. I knew if I had a girl I would be so overprotective, plus I had no experience with girls. The possibility of having a girl scared the daylights out of me. Nonetheless I wanted a baby, preferably a blue-eyed baby boy. It took a whole year for me to get pregnant much to my frustration. During that year I monitored my ovulation cycles and took my temperature, and basically tried to control getting pregnant. At one point I thought I had miscarried because I was sure I was pregnant but then my menstrual cycle started and it was different. I got quite depressed about it though and finally gave up trying to force it.

Three months later I found out I was eight weeks with child (Seth).

So upon remembering this, and my suspicions about being pregnant once upon a time and wondering if I really had lost a baby, I pulled out my pendulum.

I asked the question: "Have I ever lost a child?"
Answer: Yes.

I felt the blood draining from my face.

Next question: "Was the child I lost a girl?"
Answer: Yes.

That's when the tears flowed from my eyes as if a damn had broken. I had lost a girl and I didn't even know it. Subconsciously I must have known but was never able to mourn her. I went in search of Tyler who was playing his computer game downstairs completely unaware. It must have been difficult to understand me with all my blubbering. I think he eventually got the gist of it and comforted me as best as he could, then tucked me back into bed and told me to leave the pendulum alone for the night.

Two more weeks passed before my third session and I felt excited. I even managed to convince Tyler to book an appointment right after mine.

For fun I used Tyler as my guinea pig to see if I could check and see if his chakras were open the same way the practitioner used a pendulum on me. I got him to lie down and I held my pendulum over where I thought his chakras were. The pendulum moved in circles but then I realized I didn't know if clockwise was open or closed. I thought all his chakras were closed so when he went in for his session he was told by Patty; no, they were not all closed.

In my third Reiki session, the CD that was playing got static interference. I was told the angels were there assisting and interfering with the electronics. Patty finally got annoyed by the sound and turned it off. I thought it was funny and sweet that angels cared enough to help me during my session. We talked again about the child I lost and I asked if my daughter knew that I do love her?

"Of course!" Patty said.

Patty must have thought or known I was ready to hear it because she went on to tell me I had lost not one but two girls during my first marriage, both in the same year. Both girls were around me during my Reiki sessions and she thought maybe they were my Reiki angels. I was sad to hear this but I took the news well and found it comforting that they were still with me. I was concerned it was my fault that they weren't born, all because I wanted a boy.

"No," she said, "It doesn't work that way. If it's what's meant to be, it'll be."

After my session I had no dizziness or extra energy. I wondered if I would have side effects like I did after my first session, but I didn't and neither did Tyler. It was nice to be able to compare notes with my fiancé.

After only the first two sessions I was already convinced that I wanted to get my Reiki certification. I knew I had the capability, I just needed to find a trainer who could do the attunement on me. Lucky for me I found someone nearby, so I booked level 1 and 2 attunements, but that wouldn't take place until December. I figured that was just as well because that would allow me time to complete my Reiki sessions that I had already booked, which were for me to heal and not about becoming a practitioner.

I felt like once I had completed my Reiki training it would be best put to use it on animals. Maybe I could help some of the poor animals in the shelters. I would help my friends too, of course, but mostly animals. I saw some YouTube videos of people doing Reiki on animals and they absolutely love it. I know lots of people would benefit from it as well but I would tire of having to constantly explain how it works.

Animals trust what they feel and they know what Reiki is when they feel the healing energy. Tyler is worried that if I do that, we might need a bigger place because he may come home to a house full of animals that I HAD to rescue from the shelter. He's probably not wrong.

My fourth Reiki session was interesting. While Patty was working, out of the blue she asked me about the tattoo I was considering getting. I hadn't mentioned it to anyone, so I knew my guides were tattling on me.

"Yes," I said, "I was thinking about maybe getting symbols down the side of my rib cage."

"Well, I'm supposed to tell you to wait. That while you're writing your book a phrase will come up and you will get it tattooed down your arm. I can see it and it looks really nice!" she said, sounding quite excited about it.

"Really?" I said, unsure how I felt about that. I have two tattoos placed where I can cover them up as I see fit. Getting a tattoo on my arm didn't seem like something I would do.

"I can't see what colour it is. Hang on" she said while grabbing her pendulum.

"Is it blue? No."

"Is it red? No. Oh don't get a red tattoo. Apparently you're allergic to red ink."

"Is it black? Yes."

"How would your workplace feel about you having a tattoo on your arm?" Patty asked, knowing I have a government job.

"PFFT!" I half snorted. "I'm not concerned about what they think. IF I get a tattoo on my arm that's my choice. No one dictates to me what I can and cannot do with my body. If they're that stuffy about it, tough cookies. Anyway. I'll wait and see what this phase is first."

"They said you'll know it when you see it. Just be patient," Patty said smugly.

Be patient. They really like to stress that, don't they? I don't have a choice on this one, now do I? The last thing I want to do is get a tattoo that I will later regret. I just hope it doesn't take forever to find out what this phrase is.

CHAPTER 11

Totem Animals

If what I have been reading about and learning is true, it seems I might have one totem animal/guide with me my whole life (a wolf), and that the traits of that totem animal reflects many of my own traits, if not all, in a human way. Other totem animals will come and go and they are merely messengers for me to heed at that particular time.

I had a very strange experience as I was walking through the park on my way to a meeting in another building. This park is home to lots of animals, such as seagulls, squirrels, and various other birds. There is a huge splash park that the birds swim in and there are plenty of trees, so it's nice to walk through and enjoy nature while trekking from one place to another. As I was walking along the pathway I saw one black squirrel chasing another, which I thought was funny, so I stopped to watch them. As I was watching, the squirrel doing the chasing suddenly stopped, turned, ran closer to me, and jumped up on a cement pillar staring at me while twitching its tail. It didn't make a sound; it just stared at me. Then it ran off again. It was such odd behaviour that I couldn't ignore it, especially after being told to watch for 'signs.' So I started looking up meanings for a squirrel. I didn't fully understand what the message was, but basically squirrels are about activity and preparedness, meaning if a squirrel has scampered into your life one should examine their own activity and preparedness. I think the message was about balance, though I was not sure what I was supposed to balance.

The next totem visitor I had was while I was at work while sitting at my desk. Normally I would not have thought much about it but I am on the eighth floor and I ended up in a staring contest with a pigeon in my window. It stared at me for so long I took a picture of it. When I tried to move closer to the window it finally flew away. It crapped on my windowsill too. A few minutes later there were two more in my other window, but they didn't stay for long. Just long enough to crap in that windowsill as well.

Upon reading about pigeons I learned that they are of the dove family and are a symbol of peace, love, gentleness, maternity, and spirit messenger. Pigeons/doves are about returning to love and security of home. Once again, I was not entirely sure what the message was, except that maybe someone through the veil wanted to reach me. That in itself was positive and uplifting.

CHAPTER 12

Card Readings

I am currently the proud owner of two sets of cards. The first set I got for talking to my spirit guides is called "Messenger Oracle" by Ravynne Phelan. The second set, which are intended for talking to angels are, "Archangel Power Tarot cards" by Doreen Virtue and Radleigh Valentine.

Both sets appealed to me in their own way. I love the artwork of both sets, and the more I use them the more I know I didn't choose these cards by mistake. I still find it shocking that I can read cards for myself and know they are meant for me. Due to my inexperience, I always ask that the cards meant for me fall out or present themselves in a way that I know they are for me. My inexperience means I'm still unsure, and although I want to trust myself, I still feel clueless at times. I try not to second guess and the more the cards apply to my question or situation the easier it gets for me to trust the guidance. Most of the time, I get the same cards, or cards with similar meanings and messages.

When something significant happened or changed, I noticed the cards would change. Sometimes the messages were very reassuring, whereas other cards would confuse the daylights out of me and I would complain out loud that I had no idea what they were on about. The funny thing is I would get the clarification from another "light-worker" as we tend to be called. Or better yet, the answer would come in the form of an epiphany. When using my angel cards, I received a lot of cards from Archangel Michael and I sometimes pictured him smacking himself on the forehead in frustration trying to make me understand. *Well, too bad, it's not easy for us folk on the physical plain!*

The card which came up a few times was the "Two of Michael: It will all feel better if you make a choice." There was more, but that line was the cause of my confusion. What choice? I didn't know I had to make a choice! Then I would mutter, "Could they be any vaguer?" I must have seemed like a sullen child but I truly felt lost. I wanted to understand but I seemed to be missing something. It never did become clear to me, so I was glad when I stopped getting that card.

The best card I got from my Oracle cards was, "Card 2: Be Patient." Without even reading the rest of the card I started laughing. My spirit guides should know me better than anyone, so what made them think I was suddenly going to learn to be patient when I was excited about something? That card came up more than once but one situation they may have been referring to was when I decided I wanted to see auras. I knew other people who could see auras, which are the colours around the human body. I wanted to see them too and found tutorials online that said having a white wall behind you or the person you are reading helps. Also, you need to un-focus your eyes.

I have no white walls in my house so I attempted to stare at myself in the mirror of the bathroom and only seemed to gain eye strain and watery eyes. So in my infinite wisdom I hung a sheet on the wall behind the couch where Tyler frequently sat to play on his laptop. Then I sat on the nearby couch and stared at him. He moved around a lot and caused the sheet to fall a few times, so after tacking it back up I asked him to sit still (not an easy task for him at the best of times). I tried more staring, un-focusing until after half an hour Tyler whined that he was uncomfortable. It was sweet of him to be so patient but I gained nothing from the experience other than a headache.

So I might as well be patient....it's not like I had a choice.

Colleen from work later told me about an online app that allowed you to do card readings right on your iPhone. I downloaded it, "Path of the Soul, Destiny Cards" by Cheryl Lee Harnish. The artwork is called fractal art and it's stunning. The messages for me have been accurate and meaningful so I pull a single card every day.

CHAPTER 13

My Fun Facts

Fun Fact 1:

During my continued reading and exploration I came across a new term called, "Soul Types," also known as "spiritual archetypes." There are seven roles and they are: Priest, Server, Artisan, Warrior, King, Sage, and Scholar. I found the best explanation from www. MichaelTeachings.com

I believe myself to be a Sage, which apparently has its own vibration/tone. Each 'role' refers to the type of function we serve in the scheme of things.

SAGE: are naturally engaging, articulate, charming, entertaining, and expressive.

Everyone is one or another of these and each has their own traits. Sages excel in entertaining forms of self-expression with natural wit and wisdom.

I should show that to my mom because she always called it, "Being a smart ass."

Even though the description of the Sage loosely described me I still wasn't totally sure, so I checked with my pendulum and it said yes I was a Sage.

Fun Fact 2:

Another tip I was given by my guides through my oracle cards was "Heed your Dreams." I had heard this advice a number of times. The idea is that when you wake from a dream you are supposed to write down what it was about and any feelings associated with it. Then later, when you are more awake, you can look up the meaning in a dream dictionary or consider how the dream made you feel and what your subconscious was trying to tell you. From what I understand, the people in your dreams are not actually about those people. The people in your dreams are actors, each playing a role of your own personality, which is kind of weird if you happen to have a sex dream.

I have always had the weirdest, nonlinear, scene jumping dreams you could imagine. Oddly enough, when my awakening started, I also had the occasional dream that almost made some sense. Or at least which gave me something to look up in a dream dictionary. For example, one night I dreamt that I was either looking at buying or selling a house, but the odd thing was the fish pond in the back yard that I was very protective of. Apparently, seeing a fishpond in your dream represents subconscious material that is slowly revealing itself. Not a ground breaking message but it did positively reinforce my conscious thoughts about what I thought was happening. It also meant there was value in monitoring my dreams.

Fun Fact 3:

Regression readings are cool!
Healing Light whom I had added on Facebook had a post that caught my eye. They were having a sale on regression readings November 19, 2014 called "Who was I?" For $40 you could get an email and an MP3 of a 30 minute reading about your past life, which would be sent in three to five days. I figured I could afford to lose $40 if I didn't get anything out of it, so no harm in trying. She sent my reading via email but I will give you the condensed version of what she said.

At one time I lived in a place called Sirius. People that live there are called Sirians. She went on to say that people from Sirus often develop an early ability to see angels, spirit friends, and devas. Sirians are often very visual, both in their ability to see the things which others do not see, and also in their manner of learning. Many Sirians have a close connection with stones, crystals, and other first and second dimensional beings.

I had to look this up because I had never heard of it before. I learned that Sirus is actually a star. It's nice to know where I originated from. Actually, it was a relief to know I was not truly from here, which is maybe a strange reaction. More pieces of the puzzle were falling into place.

She said I spent a significant amount of time in Ancient Egypt and that my mother in this life was also with me in other lifetimes including my time in Egypt.

I have always been fascinated by Egypt! So after this reading I went to an Egyptian store in Calgary, to see if anything triggered a memory. No such luck, but the man running the store was very knowledgeable and spiritual. He burned something and said a prayer for me. I don't know what it was for but I appreciated his help. I ended up buying a book about Egypt and an amber necklace.

The most significant part of the Egypt book was the section on healing. They believed it was a form of 'Magic' which made me laugh. I knew this was the part which applied to me directly. I have no doubt that I spent time in a temple and in pyramids. I was a healer and healers were revered in those days. I think my time in Egypt was reasonably positive, so I think I was lucky because in those days many were sacrificed or were slaves. Although I am sure I had more than one life in Egypt, most likely not all were good.

CHAPTER 14

Spirit Fair

A spirit fair was coming to Calgary at a Casino in town and Seth and I were both excited about going. This would be our first time attending an event that would have other gifted people all in one place. A friend from work heard about it as well and we discussed meeting up there. I was most excited about meeting other light-workers but also about learning more, and hopefully making a few connections.

When we arrived we did a quick tour of the place to see how big it was and what was there. I was a little disappointed that it wasn't bigger and that there was no food/drink venue of any kind. There were a lot of card readers but since I could read my own cards I didn't think that would be money well spent. Technically, I was spending money I didn't have as it was but I felt whatever I bought would be a good investment. We barely made it halfway through our tour when I saw an Akashic records reading booth. I knew from my research that Akashic records meant accessing universal information. I had no idea that you could get readings on it though! I immediately went over and put my name down on the list for the next time slot. Then Seth and I continued with our tour. We stopped at another Akashic records reading booth only because they had some interesting crystals that caught our eye. I found a beautiful Blue Celestite with a label that read:

"Celestite: This beautiful stone is imbued with Divine energies. Celestite has a high vibration and is a teacher for the New Age. It takes you into the infinite peace of the spiritual and contacts the Angelic realms. It jumpstarts spiritual development and urges you toward enlightenment. Promotes purity of the heart and attracts good fortune. Excellent healing stone associated with the throat chakra, dissolving pain, and bringing in love."

I was very drawn to it, so for $45 I purchased it. Seth also purchased an assortment of crystals using his allowance money he had been saving for this day.

Eventually my friend caught up with us and we continued our tour. I met a lady who made lotion specifically for grounding oneself. She explained that aromatherapy is so effective because it permeates the aura instantly, which is why her beautifully scented lotion would ground you immediately when used. I'm constantly told I need to ground myself and it did smell nice, so why not? I bought a bottle from her and we chatted for a while.

At another table I met a psychic medium with 50 years experience who told me she also had healing powers. She asked me to hold out my left palm, which I did and she hovered her palm above mine. I immediately felt a coldness, so I told her. She thanked me and said it was her energy I felt, her gift. I'm not sure what she was thanking me for exactly but I liked her. While I was busy, Seth was eyeing up some more crystals at another table where a psychic was doing card readings. Seth came back all excited because the nice lady gave him the crystals for free, so I made a point of thanking her. I think they knew that Seth is a crystal child, which means he's gifted and it refers to the era in which he was born. What his gifts are I have yet to figure out, but I suspect he is a healer as well.

Finally, it was time to get my Akashic records reading with Teza Zialcita. She started with a numerology formula (which I had already done for myself) and quickly determined we had the same life path #9. She was very excited about this, which made me smile. She said she recognized my soul and we must have known each other in another lifetime. She was genuine so I believed her.

To help understand what Teza wrote down for the numerology chart, I will tell you that my full name is Kimberly-Jo Wuirch (Wuirch is my married last name), and my birth date is February 27, 1978.

This is what Teza wrote down Page 1:

2 – Co-operation / Balance
27 – 9 – Integrity / Wisdom

1978
10
<u>*15*</u>
25 = 7 – Trust / Openness

 2 + 9 + 7 = 18 = 9 – Integrity / Wisdom

Left Side
Body – back – emotional support
 throat
 neck / shoulders

Mind-

 – bars / jail
 -freedom

Spirit – sadness – grief
Energetic imprints
Soul – open

Other beings – Master Crystal Devas

None of this made much sense to me, and Seth was there distracting us with his curiosity. Teza did mention that I was the first person she had seen at the event who had Master Crystal Devas hanging around. I had no idea who the Master Crystal Devas were.

I wondered if maybe they were there with Seth and it seemed like they were with me, only because he was at my side. I figured I would review it all later and maybe it would eventually make sense.

This is what Teza wrote down, Page 2

Lessons

1. *Name your girls*
2. *Fully expressing your wisdom*
 3. *Not being hard on yourself*
4. *Creating your "light business" channel*
5. *Akashic Records Scribe*

✡ *Archangel Raziel*

Pisces
Blue Obsidian
St. Anthony

Teza asked me, "You lost two girls, yes?"

"Yes," I replied.

"Tonight, when you go home, I want you to light a candle and name your girls. Can you do that?"

"Of course yes I can do that," I said.

She didn't expand on lessons two to four, but for lesson five, she told me, "You're meant to be an Akashic Records Scribe. You must write."

"What's a scribe?" I had to ask.

"It's someone who's meant to write from the Akashic records for humanity," Teza explained.

Her explanation sort of made sense to me in that I have always wanted to write a book but I never had a topic to write about.

This is what Teza wrote down Page 3:

2 Portals

1. *Forgiveness*
2. *Release*

In all timelines, dimensions, and realities

Teza asked me to repeat three times, "I forgive myself in all timelines, dimensions, and realities those whom I have hurt intentionally or unintentionally."

Then she asked me to repeat three times, "I forgive in all timelines, dimensions, and realities those who have hurt me intentionally or unintentionally."

Teza was very patient with Seth's interruptions and she was kind to him. This concluded my reading so we got up and she gave Seth a copy of her book, *Universal Conscious Self – simple steps to connect to your true essence.* She also gave us a blue/green heart-shaped Obsidian crystal. I offered to pay for the book and crystal but she said they were gifts and she only allowed me to pay for the reading. She also mentioned that Seth and I would one day own a crystal business together. We got our pictures taken with her. I had a feeling I would be seeing her again, one day.

Seth and I were drawn to another table that also had crystals on the table, but the crystals were encased in glass, and set in glass decanters with water. They were giving samples of gem water. Since we were thirsty this was exactly what we needed so we asked to try each. First we had some plain water, then we were handed various water from decanters that had different crystal combinations. Each one tasted different. The lady providing the demo said not everyone can taste the difference but those who are gifted with crystals can always taste the different flavors. I really wanted one or two or all but even one was out of my price range. So I took the pamphlet and thanked her. She mentioned the website and gave me her business card.

I went to her side table where she had an assortment of jewelry and other loose crystals. I picked one up and it zapped me. I squeaked and set it down complaining that it had zapped me and the sales lady giggled. When my friend came over she picked up the same crystal that zapped me and she wanted it. It didn't zap her, so I guess she was meant to have it, and I prodded her to purchase it. Seth purchased a book called *Gem Water* by Michael Gienger and Joachim Goebel. I know if ever I get the chance (and enough crystals) I want to make my own gem water.

All in all we had a great time and we got plenty of treasures to take home.

Back at home I had to look up what Master Crystal Devas were. From what I read there is a Crystal Kingdom which is guarded by a group of feminine beings known as Crystal Devas. They oversee crystal deposits on Earth as well as other realms. I will have to look more into that later, if I end up using crystals once I get my Reiki training. Or if Seth and I really do go into a crystal business together. Only time will tell.

CHAPTER 15

Body Talk

I had been asking around about how I could safely get off my depression medication. I knew I no longer needed the medication, but when I asked my medical doctor to reduce them he said it was better to wait until spring. I understood why, because people are very susceptible to depression in the wintertime but I knew it wasn't right for me personally anymore. So when he refused I was very disappointed. The more I thought about it the more I knew I did not need the medication any longer and I felt it was hindering me spirituality. Of course I couldn't tell my doctor that. I also knew I could not go off the medication cold turkey as that would be dangerous, especially with the dosage I was on. I was told to get a body talk session because Reiki could not help me with this. So I booked someone who came highly recommended, whom I will call Violet.

I was unsure what to expect so I looked it up on the internet. The explanation provided meant very little to me. It said something about transferring data from my head to my heart. I wasn't concerned about it. I just needed to know how to get off my meds as safely as possible. When I got there I filled out some paperwork about myself and then I was asked a few questions while Violet made notes and then she asked me to lie on the bed/table. Once I was settled, Violet put one hand on my head and the other on my side and closed her eyes. She asked questions about my family, which can be very confusing to try and explain.

Basically, starting with biological parents there is my mom and my biological dad. I never knew my biological father and he doesn't know I exist. My mom knew him for a short time and once they parted ways they never saw each other again and he never knew my mom was pregnant. I used to know his name but have since forgotten. I assume my blue eyes came from him. During my mom's pregnancy with me she met someone new, with whom my mom had two boys, my brothers. That's the extent of my immediate family. My brother's dad was only around until I was five or six.

I explained all this to Violet as best I could, which in turn helped her figure out that someone on my biological dad's side of the family, about four generations back, had been incarcerated, tied up, and abused. Whatever happened had come down through the genes to me through DNA and this connection was affecting me negatively. Violet said she could see bars over my heart. She told me she would help by cutting that tie.

Remember the Akashic record reading? Heart – bars/jail. Freedom.

Now it made sense. Another puzzle piece fit neatly into place. *Click!*

Violet also found the tension in my neck. My neck had been so tight and sore and no amount of massage or hot baths seemed to help. I had tried everything I could think of but nothing worked! Violet said it was a seed of anger that had gotten trapped there. She said she could release it and she did. It immediately felt better. Not 100 percent better right away, but it did start to ease immediately. It healed over the next week, which was such a relief.

She also balanced my feminine and masculine energies. I had no clue what that meant but thanks anyway if that's what I needed! She balanced my elements (don't ask me). Then she used crystal singing bowls, which was weird because the sound moved from one ear to the other and back and forth. I mentioned this and she exclaimed, "Oh, you can hear that?"

"Yes, can't everyone?" I said.

"Nope, not everyone notices it moving from one side to the other," she stated.

She continued my session with tuning forks to do some healing in my jaw, and she sensed tension in my hip. I've had trouble with that hip for years but it only ever aggravated me when I was jogging or running. What Violet saw there was a terrified little girl (me) curled up in the fetal position, frightened and alone (THAT I knew was from my childhood). So she said she would put down a ladder for the little girl to climb up and once she was at the top the ladder was removed. She told me she saw that my older self was exited to show this little girl around.

She saw a lioness (would have to look that up later).

She also said I had put heavy duty barriers and protection up when I was a child. There was a protection over my eyes that she was going to remove for me as I didn't need it anymore. I was an adult now and I was safe. The barriers could come down and the protection could be removed.

At the end of the session I asked about the depression medication I was on. "Oh," she said, "I'll give you a couple of products to take along with instructions. After three days of it being in your system you can start reducing your medication."

"How will I know how much to reduce by and when?" I asked worriedly.

"You're intuitive, so you will know," she said with a smile.

With that Violet hugged me and told me she was leaving for Egypt in a few days and then she sent me on my way.

As soon as I saw my mom that evening, I told her all about the session, but especially about what came down through the DNA.

"That makes sense," my mom said. "His family was living in Germany some generations back during the time of Hitler when all that stuff happened with the Jewish people."

Yikes. I didn't ask for details.

That left looking up what a lioness totem animal meant. Here is the short version of what I found:

Female lions are the best hunters and do most of the hunting and child rearing, which can mean the assertion of feminine energies to bring forth new power. Trust feminine energies – creativity, intuition, and imagination. Don't worry about whether you will succeed. Instead, go after what you desire. Your intuitive side will strengthen as you develop the skill of sensing what is around you and knowing exactly when to make your move.

CHAPTER 16

Vibration

One word that comes up a lot is "vibration" and "raising your vibration."

To the best of my understanding, there are different levels of vibration. Dense vibrations are heavier, while less dense vibrations are lighter. At least to our way of experiencing these vibrations. Our bodies and this physical plane of existence are considered very dense. When we leave our physical bodies the experience is much lighter and less dense. Some people describe our bodies and the earth as low vibration and the spirit realm which is not physical as high vibration. It's not that one is bad and the other is good. It's simply the best way to explain the duality.

I decided I wanted to raise my vibration since this seemed to be what everyone was striving for if they were spiritual. I found these charts which showed that certain emotions such as shame, guilt, grief, and fear had very low vibrational frequencies, which are measured in Hertz. Emotions like love, peace, joy, and happiness were on the high end of the vibrational frequencies.

Food was also listed in charts with different vibrational frequencies. Canned, processed, and genetically modified foods measured 0 on the Hertz scale. Some of the foods that were low on the vibrational chart surprised me, like aquatic bottom feeders, game meats, and pork. Red meat was only slighter higher than those, and mid-range included eggs, chicken, fowl, fish, and dairy. Highest vibrational foods were vegetables, fruits, living grains, and nuts.

No wonder so many spiritual people were vegans and vegetarians! I thought it was because these poor people could feel the energy of the animals when they died, but maybe it was more than that. Just my luck too that I've always lived on meat and Tyler is a hunter who provides us with a freezer full of meat once a year. He saves us a fortune on groceries and I thought it was healthier. I could go days without eating meat and I would prefer to, but Tyler eats it every day.

Other items that are said to be vibrationally low are sugar, caffeine, alcohol, and chocolate. The obvious ones like drugs and smoking are not an issue as I've never been a smoker or drug user. The only good news was that wine and beer have a high vibration and are considered a food, however excess has the opposite effect. So moderation is key if you enjoy wine and/or beer.

Even music has high and low vibrations. Heavy metal and rap supposedly vibrates at 40/1000 Hertz. 432 Hertz is supposed to transmit beneficial healing energy because it is mathematically consistent with the Universe.

The only way I could verify any of this was to try it. If it was true it should make me healthier and happier, and maybe a higher vibration would make it easier to talk to my spirit guides. Chocolate is easy for me to stop eating since it often has dairy in it and I'm allergic to dairy. Tyler quit drinking, so not only could I be supportive by not drinking, but I would be cutting out calories and raising my vibration at the same time. Sugar? Let's not be hasty! I'll take that one a little slower and cut back a little. I decided to start incorporating more raw and whole foods into my diet, and stop buying so many processed foods. I would need to find new recipes that I liked. Eating healthily is a lot more expensive, and while I do prefer organic foods we'll see how much my pocket book allows.

When listening to my music I realized I did have songs that were rather depressing, or had rapping in the chorus, and I did sometimes listen to heavy rock on the radio. Nothing that I am so attached to that I can't stop listening to it, especially considering the vast and various options for music available to us these days.

Now I have a mission! Good Vibrations :)

CHAPTER 17

Ringing Ears

I recently started experiencing ringing in my ears. At first I didn't think much of it. It wasn't painful, nor did it last very long. It wasn't always in the same ear, nor was it always the same pitch. It didn't bother me at all, so I ignored it. The explanation I heard was that it was the little hairs in your ears dying, so I briefly thought I would be losing my hearing because I had listened to rock music too loud when I was younger. Then I remembered reading that the ringing was sometimes information being downloaded to the subconscious from the Akashic Records. I also recall it as being one of the "symptoms" of spiritual awakening.

That was all well and good until the pitch changed one day while I was at work. It became much higher and I got a feeling of urgency that I simply could not ignore. Something changed, but what the heck was it? I went onto one of the Facebook groups I had joined and posted a question about it. As usual I received various responses, but the one that caught my attention was that someone was trying to give me a message. Still, if someone was trying to give me a message, I couldn't understand them. All I heard was BZZZZZZZZZ, which is a fat lot of good. It happened at different times of the day for a few days.

I had a Reiki appointment with Patty that weekend so I mentioned it.

Using her pendulum Patty asked:

"Is someone trying to give Kim a message?"
Yes.
"Is it a family member?"
No.
"Is it someone from this lifetime?"
Yes.

So that only confirmed my suspicions, but it didn't help much. I hadn't lost many people I was close to except for my "step" grandfather on my brother's side of the family. I was always close to him and I adored him. With the chaos that was my family life I didn't always get to see him, sometimes not for years. When she asked if it was a family member, I kind of hoped it was him but the pendulum said no it's not family. I was quite disappointed by that.

On my drive home it occurred to me that maybe the pendulum is very literal. I mean, it would have to be, as it doesn't have a mind of its own. So if it was my "grandfather," technically he was not a blood relative because he was JJ's father. I always called him Grandfather, like my brothers did. Rhonda might know, so I sent her a message on Facebook. This was the conversation (and LOL means laugh out loud for those who don't know):

ME: *"Hey Rhonda, are you able to tune into whoever has been trying to talk to me from the other side? In Reiki I found out it was someone from this lifetime. I think it was my "step" grandfather known to me as John. The problem is, I only hear buzzing in my ears but can't understand. If you can help I will find some way to repay you. Thank you"*

Rhonda: *"Have you asked him to speak clearer? Buzzing is normal and soooo irritating, lol."*

Me: *"Yes, I tried that but I'm not attuned enough yet and the buzzing is happening daily. I told whoever it was I can't understand."*

Rhonda: *"It's male energy, older gentleman – that much I'm picking up. He's gesturing to me and shrugs. Did this man kinda walk hunched over?"*

Me: *"Maybe at the end because he had stomach cancer. That's what killed him."*

Rhonda: *"Ok, you are making me tingle, lol, good energy though! He has an important message. I'm asking him to communicate on a lower frequency you can understand."*

Me: *"Ha, he's been trying hard to talk to me, that much I gathered. Otherwise I wouldn't pester you."*

Rhonda: *"I'm giving him the lower frequency talk. He's sorry."*

Me: *"Aww!"*

Rhonda: *"He said you're a sweetie and not to let anyone take advantage, follow your gut and instincts. Girl you're talented, you are opening Pandora's Box, all good things coming! He was waiting for Tyler to come back to you, he's happy your happy!' He has more to tell you but I'm only getting small bits."*

Rhonda: *"Your circle of friends will change. Keep going along, you will find out more about you than you realized."*

Me: *"Thank you, Rhonda. I will repay you in kind. I miss him so much every day."*

Rhonda: *"No need, happy to help dear."*

Me: *"Maybe now my ears will stop buzzing so much! Lol, or they will buzz even more!"*

Rhonda: *"Lol"*

Me: *"I can't thank you enough."*

Rhonda: *"You're welcome."*

I thought I had handled that conversation very well. I read the entire conversation to Tyler who took it all in stride as well. Then the damn broke and I cried.

"I miss him," I said to Tyler.

"I know baby, I know you do," Tyler replied softly while hugging me.

Even as I type this, the tears well up again.

Once I was calm I said to Tyler, "You know, the movie 'The Sixth Sense' probably would not have been very good if it was based on real life."

"Oh yeah, why's that?" he asked

"Because the kid would have said, 'I hear dead people, it sounds like BZZZZZZZZZ!'"

It doesn't have the same effect.

It might help if I explain that my grandfather died when I was 19 years old and I never got to say goodbye and there was no funeral. I simply got a call from one of his daughters informing me of his passing. At the time I had no idea that he was dying because he kept it from me and probably all his grandkids that he was sick.

What is also significant to note is that Tyler and I were childhood sweethearts. I met Tyler when I was 13 years old and Tyler was 16. I was smitten the second I met him. We both hung out with the same friends, and by the time I was 14 and he was 17, we were a couple. Sadly, a year later my stepdad and stepmother moved us out of town and out of school making it challenging for me to see Tyler, but he still managed to spend time with me anyway. Six months after that I was moved into the middle of nowhere to live on a trap line, to be homeschooled at age 15. Tyler made it all the way out there twice but the distance and lack of roads made it nearly impossible to remain a couple. At age 16, right on my birthday as a matter of fact, I moved out. I'd had enough, so I had called my mom who was living in

Calgary at the time and asked her to drive to northern Alberta to get me. Without hesitation she did, putting even more distance between Tyler and I. Once I had settled in I had called all my friends, including Tyler and my grandfather to let them all know where I was living now. It wasn't until I was 17 that I saw Tyler again. I decided to jump on a greyhound bus one weekend and cross the many miles to see him. It was that weekend I realized we could not be together. I had too much to accomplish and he could not come with me. So we parted ways not knowing if we'd ever see each other again.

It wasn't until tragedy struck Tyler the day after my 34th birthday that I found my way back to him, 17 years later. So when my grandfather said he was waiting for Tyler to come back to me it appeared it was predestined?

Needless to say, when the ringing started again I naturally assumed it was my grandfather again, so I texted Rhonda:

Me: *"Someone is trying to talk to me again. They are back to ringing my ear. No clue if it's Grandpa or someone else? Ring ring. Hello? Buzzzzzz."*

Rhonda: *"Lol. I'm picking up female."*

Me: *"Female now?"*

Rhonda: *"Ugh! They said they will stop once you're more attuned... I know you can do more, I can feel it. There's something about you that I'm so comfy talking to you about this! Yes, there are two names being presented to me, 'Mary and Wendy'. Do either mean anything to you?"*

Me: *"Jesus's mom? LOL! Sorry no. Neither mean anything."*

Rhonda: *"Lol, ok just putting forth names spirit gave me."*

Me: *"Well aren't they helpful. Not. My mom doesn't know the names either."*

Rhonda: *"No? Bummer. Now someone is buzzing at me!"*

Me: *"BAH HA HA HA HA!*

Rhonda: *"I think as you progress you will be able to hear and see like me."*

Me: *"Yeah, my cards keep saying how powerful I am and I'm trying. I need to raise my vibration more."*

Seven months passed and I had not heard from my grandfather again and it hasn't been for a lack of trying on my part. I can only assume he is happy where he is. That will have to be enough.

I got the buzzing in my ears for a number of months but never again felt like it was someone trying to give me a message.

CHAPTER 18

Angel Messages

This chapter is a conversation Rhonda and I had one evening through Facebook and it is the only reason I considered publishing this book. Originally I wrote my journal for my son who I suspected was a healer and gifted like me. I wanted to make sure that if anything ever happened to me before I had the chance to guide him or help him through the transition that I could at least leave a journal for him both as a keepsake and a guide. I never wanted him to think he was crazy or feel alone or ashamed that he was different, and my journal was assurance that if one day I wasn't there to tell him in person, my journal would do it for me.

Here is our conversation:

Me: *"If you have a moment, someone is babbling at me in the high pitch again and I told them to lower the vibration but nothing happened. Sorry to be a pain."*

Rhonda: *"I'm picking up two."*

Me: *"Two again?! No wonder it was so high pitch!"*

Rhonda: *"Male and female. The female is waving her hands and pointing at a paper. Important info on that paper you need to find it."*

Me: *"Must be my journal I have in my hands. I'm turning it into a novel."*

Rhonda: *"The male is trying to help you but he can't understand why you can't hear him. She says yes, I'm to tell you to keep writing"*

Me: *"Ok fine, I was only distracted for a minute while I was looking for a Pisces symbol. LOL!*

Rhonda: *"She says you need to journal, it's important."*

Me: *"Ok thank you so much. It seemed urgent."*

Rhonda: *"You are the key! LOL. I'm laughing because she shows me a key and you are going to help many people with their reservations about empathy. Empaths."*

Me: *"Ah, I can see that."*

Rhonda: *"They keep showing me a white rose too."*

Me: *"Not sure. I'm sure it will click eventually. I'm sure lucky to have you as a friend."*

Rhonda: *"It's what I do. I have to balance right? So this is my way of repayment."*

Me: *"Lucky for me, I still really appreciate it a lot. Can I mention you in my book? You can have an alias if you want."*

Rhonda: *"I'm seeing a road to many opportunities coming for you, the book is the beginning.*

I don't mind, you can use my name."

Me: *"Wow, profound. Cool! You will be famous! ;)"*

Rhonda: *"That would tickle me pink. Brought a tear."*

Me: *"Aww."*

Rhonda: *"Anyways, umm, spirit is pulling you into a new direction, as you grow things will become clearer! These two are here to help guide you. They need to lower their frequency!"*

Me: *"UH, YEAH!"*

Rhonda: *"Also we need to find a course, they are adamant about it."*

Me: *"Course for what? I'm taking Reiki. Maybe you need to as well?"*

Rhonda: *"Maybe. She's showing me light and hands."*

Me: *"Yup that's Reiki! You have to take it too. Haha! Maybe my Reiki trainer can add you for the same dates as me."*

Rhonda: *"You should feel how scary energetic my hands get. It scares me!"*

Me: *"Make an energy ball and see if you can start a fire. LOL! I know I'm so helpful."*

Rhonda: *"Pfft, no problem."*

Me: *"No matches :)"*

Rhonda: *"She's telling me Seth is a healer too. That's why he and Logan connect so well."*

Me: *"Yeah, I knew he was."*

Rhonda: *"There's something about the one book and crystals she's really excited you're going write. Something about it has to do with Seth. I'm not sure if he helps you or if he inspires you to write it...."*

Me: *"Yeah, he's involved somehow because we supposedly do something with crystals together. At least that's what I was told."*

Rhonda: *"Interesting."*

Me: *"Yup and we end up doing work with animals together too. It looks like my future is planned."*

Rhonda: *"That's funny because she was showing me animals. If you have writer's block she says she can help with that."*

Me: *"Ok thanks."*

Rhonda: *"Not sure where the man went but he left."*

Me: *"What's her name?"*

Rhonda: *"Rachel is what she is telling me. She's calling herself a writing angel."*

Me: *"Oh, cool!"*

Rhonda: *"Maybe that's why they're speaking so fuzzy. It's because they are angels but you would think when asked they would lower their frequency."*

Me: *"I don't know why they are all so confused that I can't hear them. I was just at Reiki today. I am grounded. I don't know why I can't hear either."*

Rhonda: *"Give it time it will come. There's an earth angel book that I found that I'm to show you. I'll have to go digging. Doreen Virtue wrote it."*

Me: *"Hmm, I may have seen it on iBooks but didn't order it yet."*

Rhonda: *"It's about how to be kind but not a doormat, lol."*

Me: *"Oh that one. I kind of ignored it but ok. So I have to write a book, read a book, work and learn Reiki. Gee, my life is so boring. Oh well, who needs sleep anyway."*

Rhonda: *"LOL! I'm so excited about Reiki!"*

Me: *"Me too."*

CHAPTER 19

—◆—✴—◆—

Reiki 1 and 2 Lessons

I was so excited to be getting my Reiki I attunement. I wasn't totally sure what to expect but I knew I wanted to be able to use my hands to heal others. Rhonda was taking the lesson with me so at least I had a friend with me to share the experience with.

Our instructor worked out of her home and had a room dedicated for her Reiki business. There turned out to be four students and one instructor. I will assign fake names to protect their identities.

The first thing we received was a handout that explained all the basics. There was certainly too much to memorize in one day of training, so I was grateful for the booklet.

Next, our instructor Jessie took each student one at a time into the room designated for Reiki sessions. There was a chair in the centre of the room for the student to sit in while the attunement took place. I don't know what happened because Jessie stood behind me. I didn't feel any different, nor did I notice any change. When Jessie was done and left the room, I sat and pondered for a moment wondering if it had worked, and then got up and went back to the kitchen table. When everyone had their attunement we were told we would be spending the rest of the day doing Reiki on each other as practice.

William was my first client. First I asked him if it was okay that I touched him. Not a requirement at all, but it is nice if they say yes because it means you can rest your hands/arms on them on the less personal body parts. That way my arms wouldn't get tired being as I wasn't used to this yet. He said he would prefer it so that he knew where I was. I won't describe everything that happened but I did see a buck (male deer) while working on him. I knew this to be a totem animal and told him about it when we were done because he fell asleep during the session. Jessie said it's a great honour to have someone fall asleep on your table. She didn't elaborate why that is so I assumed it meant the person on the table trusted you (or they were exhausted).

Next, I worked on Rhonda. I asked her the same question, "Is it okay if I touch you?" She said it was fine. I tried doing Reiki on her but she was blocking me. I could feel that the energy wasn't going anywhere. I quietly told her she needed to relax because she was blocking me.

"I'm trying," she said.

I knew right away what the issue was. Even though on a conscious level she thought she was ok with my touching her, on a subconscious level she wasn't ok with it. So I took my hands off of her and hovered over the area I needed to work on, and it started to work.

When it was my turn to be on the table, Rhonda worked on me. The only thing that was memorable to me was Rhonda complaining that her hands were ice cold from working on me. That working on me was like working over an ice block. I laughed because all I felt was warmth.

Finally, I worked on Phyllis. My first impression of her was that she had spent a lot of her life in a very unhappy state of mind. I noticed there seemed to be an intense prickly feeling when working on her jaw and her left hand. I found if I stayed on that area long enough the prickly feeling would ease up and become warm. I had the impression of something bothering her and decided I would ask her afterward. Besides, she fell asleep too, as I could tell by her light snoring.

When Jessie said it was time to stop I gently nudged Phyllis awake and asked how she felt. She told me when I had first started she felt a pair of hands on her neck but I was working down by her side and she could clearly see where I was. I figured it was her Reiki guide helping me but I kept that to myself because I wasn't sure. I then asked her if she had issues with her teeth, to which she answered, "Yes, always." That explained the issues with her jaw. Then I asked if she had problems with her left hand, to which she said, "Yes, arthritis." So that made sense too.

Then more quietly I asked her if she was having difficulty forgiving herself for decisions she had made in her past? She told me yes, that she had done things she regretted. I immediately told her I didn't need the details but that if it helped I could share what had helped me overcome a similar mindset. I explained that before we incarcerated, we all planned out our lives. We made soul agreements with other people who would be in our lives to assist us with learning the lessons we were here to learn. So it seemed silly to be mad at myself for something I had mapped out for a reason. When we got here we weren't supposed to know what those plans entailed otherwise we would never truly learn the lessons. This brought tears to her eyes and instantly I felt bad for upsetting her. Still, I was sure she needed to hear it.

During that week I was still curious about what we felt while performing Reiki. I knew the warm, prickly, and cold sensations had to mean something, but what? I found differing opinions on the internet that didn't satisfy my question, so I asked my messenger friend at work. The answer I got was heat means the healing energy was going in, cold meant blocked energy was being drawn out, and tingly meant don't move from that spot until the tingling had stopped. Now that made sense. So if Rhonda thought I felt like an iceberg, I clearly had a lot of energy healing I needed to do.

My Reiki II lesson took place exactly one week after Reiki I and Rhonda was taking this lesson with me as well. Many people will tell you that you should allow 30 days in between Reiki I and Reiki II. That you need time to heal between levels and it's too much if you do it close together. Well, that's a matter of opinion and a complete generalization. First of all, I knew what I was getting into taking both so close together. I didn't need anyone telling me what was best for me or what I could and could not handle. I am a strong willed, physically healthy individual with the intelligence to decide for myself. Of course, it helps if you are given the information and allowed to decide for yourself. In my case, I did my research beforehand.

So Reiki II, which was also taught by Jessie, surprisingly had all the same students.

It was nice to be with a group of people who understood this spiritual lingo that I was getting more familiar with every day. I learned from Jessie that anything that grows from the earth will help to ground you because it is of the earth. Like carrots and potatoes, for example. She also showed us that we can use our pendulums to clear and charge our crystals, which I thought was so cool. My biggest surprise, however, was when Phyllis walked in looking happier, almost as if a huge weight had been lifted off her. I told her that her energy was much improved since the previous week and she agreed she was doing better.

We sat at the table discussing Reiki but I was having difficulty concentrating, sitting still or shutting up. I'm told this is a sign that you are not grounded, so I must have been flying high. Jessie gave me a couple of crystals to help me calm down and we settled in to do the first long distance Reiki practice. The idea was that each person would ask for a place or person to have Reiki performed on by all in attendance. Phyllis got to go first and asked that we do a clearing on her new house and property. Unfortunately, I must have missed the directions because I was so loopy and ended up sitting there doing nothing, because quite frankly I didn't know what I was supposed to be doing. With nothing to picture and no address I had no idea how to even picture the place. When we went around the circle for everyone to share their experience, I apologized that I wasn't any help and had nothing to share.

I recall having much the same experience in school, never having any clue why I could rarely concentrate. I would try so hard. I would sternly tell myself to pay attention and then drift off five minutes later. If I was listening to someone with a monotone voice I would drift off in less than a minute. Sometimes doodling would help (on paper, on my jeans, on my shoes, on my hand) but in many of my classes I would get in trouble for that. I could be staring right at the teacher the entire class and not hear a single word they said. It's amazing I got through school with passing grades.

William was next and he asked us to perform long distance Reiki on his daughter. I still wasn't convinced that you could do Reiki from a distance but I wanted to try. So I asked what his daughter's name was and then closed my eyes while focusing on her name and thinking of her as William's daughter. An image of a young girl with slightly longish black hair in a ponytail, wearing a backpack, walking away from me popped into my head. In my mind I asked for her permission to do Reiki on her. I thought I got a nod, so I proceeded. Nothing else spectacular happened but when we ended I asked if the image I had of her was accurate. William said it was.

As we were talking about what we saw and felt I was getting colder and colder. I put my jacket on, but the next thing I knew I was shaking so hard my teeth were chattering together like I was in shock. Rhonda grabbed my hand and said it was like ice so she tried to help me warm my hands. I was clueless about what was happening to me and Jessie didn't offer any explanation so I assumed she didn't know either. After about five minutes the shaking stopped and I was just cold.

Last to go was Jessie and she asked for us to work on her daughter. Her daughter is a fully grown adult and I was not comfortable doing Reiki on someone I wasn't sure would want it and who hadn't actually asked for it. So instead I chose to focus on the home her daughter lived in. I went from room to room but immediately noticed I had a tag along. A small grey and white cat was following me from room to room. I'm not sure why it was there but it wasn't interfering, so the cat and I cleared most of the house.

I asked her, "Do they have a cat?"

"Yes," she said.

"Any chance it's a grey and white cat?"

"Yes, I believe so," she replied.

"Well, their cat followed me around."

"Interesting. Okay thanks," she said.

During practice I paired up with Rhonda. I knew this time it was best to stay hands off so I did. I asked for her Reiki guides to help me with her session, not realizing I would see them, or that her Reiki guide would be a fairy. I had my eyes closed but what I saw in my mind's eye was a little fairy similar to what I've seen in cartoons or movies. It was about four inches and had wings like a dragonfly. In my head, I would show the fairy what hand positions I would do next and she would move so we were not working in the exact same spot. When I was working on Rhonda's leg, I had one hand on her hip and one on her ankle (she's short), while the fairy straddled her knee in the cutest way. The fairy stayed put while I slowly moved my hands together toward the knee. I gave the fairy an image of my putting my hands together over the fairy's head to ask if that was ok. The response was hilarious; the fairy waved her hands over her head and shook her head no. It was hard not to laugh.

As I write this I realize how ridiculous it sounds. If it was all in my head then so be it. Maybe I have a really good imagination! If I leave it out, it would be a lie by omission because if what I saw was what other people see too, they need to know they are not alone. Empaths are sensitive enough as it is without people judging them and telling them they are crazy.

Rhonda had told me before that she sees fairies. It's not that I didn't believe her, I just didn't think I would ever see one. I'm pretty sure if she hadn't told me she had seen them too I would have disregarded what popped into my head. It's not strange to me that I'm seeing and hearing things that other people can't. What's strange is that I'm okay with it all.

CHAPTER 20

Belief Re-Patterning

The Wednesday after Reiki II, I was still wracking my brain trying to understand what happened to me that caused me to get so cold it made my whole body shake and my teeth chatter. With no explanation offered by our trainer after the Reiki session, I assumed she didn't know or she would have told me. I decided to figure it out for myself. At first I assumed it had to do with whatever was in that house. Was I psychically attacked? My friend Colleen was in Las Vegas until Wednesday and I didn't want to bother her while she was on vacation. So as a last resort I posted what happened on a Facebook group. As always everyone was supportive and wanted to help but no one had the same answer and nothing they said seemed to fit. So I was still at a loss, making assumptions and jumping to any conclusion that fit. I was still a little freaked out by it and not knowing what was going on bothered me. Finally, Wednesday came and my friend was back at work. Immediately, I told her what happened. I was lectured for not properly protecting myself and all she could tell me was that there was something black around me and she had to shield herself from me. I couldn't see anything, so how was I supposed to know?! Now I was worried of putting others at risk. What if some dark energy had attached itself to me? I was told that can happen if there are tears in your aura.

More stressed than ever, I called Patty who had performed Reiki on me four times to date and had always made herself available by texting me and telling me to call anytime I needed. I told her everything that happened and asked if a Reiki session would help. She didn't believe it would, but she knew someone who might be able to help. She knew someone that did Belief Re-Patterning and promised to send me her contact information. She didn't explain why she thought Belief Re-Patterning would help and I had never heard of it before but I was desperate to try anything. That afternoon I got on the phone with Angie and I described everything that had happened. Angie believed that doing the Reiki I and II so close together had caused an intense healing to take place, which probably triggered the reaction. There was nothing attached to me, but rather the negative energy was coming FROM me as I healed spiritually, mentally, and physically. What a relief! I knew there might be consequences to taking the attunements so close together, but I didn't know what those consequences would look like. As long as I wasn't putting others at risk being around me, then I could handle it. So I booked a Belief Re-Patterning session with her for that evening hoping to speed up this healing process.

Then I sent a message to Jessie and told her what had happened since the weekend and she offered to do a Light Body Integration on me. I didn't know what that was but I said yes. I didn't feel like waiting months for all this healing to happen on its own. I wanted to get it over with already! I remembered Patty telling me I had a lot more to heal than most people, both from this life and previous lives, and that maybe this was the lifetime I was going to do it in. Fine by me, bring it on.

That evening via Skype I learned what Belief Re-Patterning was. The explanation I was given was that prior to the age of seven, everything a child learns goes straight to their subconscious. Also, prior to the age of seven everything is taken literally because during those years a child is unable to comprehend sarcasm. What you learn becomes part of your belief system. What you believe about yourself and the world around you.

Thinking back on my childhood, I wondered if one session would be enough...

The idea of Belief Re-Patterning is that you take negative words from the subconscious and turn them into new words with a positive outlook. I wish I had recorded my session but I didn't. I did, however, take some notes. I jotted down the words I was told needed to be changed and I wrote down the replacement words. Various aches and pains cropped up during the session that I told Angie about and each one seemed to mean something to her, so she used the information to help me further.

Here are the words that came up for me personally:

CURRENT WORD	NEW WORD
Violated	Survivor
Vexed	Serene
Grotesque	Proud
thirsty (for knowledge)	deserving of
Vicious	Compassion
Turmoil	Harmony

Here are the expressions of validation I need to use from now on.

I am validating...
I give myself permission...
I choose to be...
I experience freedom...
What do I want to feel instead...?

It was also recommended that I read a book written by Dan Millman called *The Laws of Spirit* which is about the 12 laws, and apparently I needed to focus on #10, The Law of Cycles. I didn't read the book right away but I do get back to it later on.

I only referred to my notes a few times after that session but I can honestly say *everything* has helped me so far because I am so much calmer, happier, no mood swings, and even my family has commented on the difference. I can think more clearly and my thoughts are certainly a lot more positive. If being crazy has made me a better person then no one around me is complaining!

CHAPTER 21

The Power of Angels

Since my previous reading through Healing Light was so cool, I thought I would see what other readings they were offering. I selected the "Akashic Karma Clearing Session" and the "Meet Your Guidance Team Reading." The Akashic Karma Clearing is supposed to help to heal from past lives and the guidance team reading would give me some actual names of those helping me from "the other side" as I prefer to call it. After that message from my grandpa, it left no doubt in my mind that there was another side and that they were trying to help me.

I was surprised when Teri Van Horne emailed me a couple of hours later to book my session and provide some instructions. She generally does the Akashic Clearing late in the evening while the person is resting or asleep. All I had to do was relax and not drink alcohol or eat a lot of red meat. I was already relaxing while watching Ellen and I hadn't had alcohol or red meat at all that day, so I asked if she wanted to do it that night and she said yes.

Once my show was over, I thought I should do everything I could to be as relaxed as possible to ensure I got my money's worth out of the clearing session. So I went upstairs to draw a hot bath and I dumped lots of Epsom salts into the water to make sure I cleansed any negative energies. I added some essential oils and candles and turned off the lights. While soaking I figured I would try to meditate again. If nothing else I would be relaxed even if it didn't work. So I closed my eyes and attempted a variation of a meditation that was suggested in one of Doreen Virtue's books, *Earth Angels*.

In my mind, I was on the beach with Seth and we were picking up shells as we love to do. When we were done Seth went to play and I dropped my shells on a beach towel, dried off, and threw a cover on. I walked over to where I had pictured a spiral staircase on the beach and stood at the bottom stair, considering my next move. Then slowly I made my way up the stairs in no hurry whatsoever. When I got to the top there was a door with a gold doorknob and a gold knocker, and light seemed to be coming out along the seam of the door. It seemed rude to barge in so I used the knocker. The door opened, seemingly of its own accord, but just a few inches. I slowly opened it the rest of the way. The room was dark at first because my eyes had to adjust. The first thing I noticed was that the floor was gleaming pink and there was a large beautiful table in the centre of the room. At first I thought I was alone but then I noticed yellow eyes near me, and I knew it was Julia my Wolf guide. I reached out a hand and patted her head, and then I hugged her, glad she was there.

The room seemed too plain to me, so I decided to decorate it myself. It seemed appropriate to hang a picture of Jesus on one wall, then a picture of Buddha on another wall. I turned around to address the next wall, but there was already a huge picture there. I had not put that there! It had a gold frame and it was larger than life-size. In the picture there was a fully grown female angel with white wings and she was sitting on grass with both her legs folded to one side. With her was a small child also sitting with her, but I couldn't focus on the child. The picture wasn't clear enough and in trying to look at it I started to cry. Not surprisingly, crying broke my meditation so I drained the tub and crawled into bed, puzzled over what had happened. Tyler was away for work, so I was alone and soon drifted off to sleep.

The next morning while driving to work, I thought back to the picture I saw of the angel and child again. The meaning of it was not clear to me and I was still trying to sort it out. To my complete surprise when I tried to picture it I started crying again, even harder. I don't cry for no reason. I'm not an outwardly emotional person at the best of times let alone for what seemed to me like no reason. I was totally out of sorts when I got to work and immediately sought out my friend Colleen who is a messenger. As soon as she saw me she asked what was wrong. I told her about the meditation the night before and why I was doing it. She nodded and smiled and told me what was happening.

Basically she told me I had needed to see that image to start the healing process, so that the Akashic Karma Clearing Session would work for me. That I had started closing the door on all spirituality when I was four, and then again at the age of seven due to trauma. The image let me know that even though I had blocked them out, the angel had been with me my whole life. The angel understood it was because of the trauma and not my fault.

Well, that broke the damn again and tears ran down my face. I knew what had happened at the age of four. I knew also, that at the age of seven I had said, "Why should I believe in a god or angels who won't protect me! If none of you will help me, then I don't need you and I don't believe in you."

To a terrified child of extreme abuse, it's perfectly understandable that I would look for someone to lash out at. This was my way of regaining some semblance of control over my life.

Remember that terrified little girl that was found in the Body Talk session? The one in the fetal position? The one that put up barriers and protection? Well that was me at seven years of age. I put that so-called protection over my eyes because I didn't want to see the angels who I blamed. I put up those emotional barriers to keep the angels and my guides from talking to me, and to stop me from shutting down emotionally. I remembered everything as if it was yesterday and I was so sorry I had done it. I was sorry I had shut them out. I know why I did it, and they know why I did it. I felt so alone because of it and their message to me was that I was NEVER alone.

Later that day I got my Akashic Karma Clearing Session feedback from Teri. She said she cleared my chakras and balanced my masculine and feminine energies. Then she removed blockages stemming from the past. What I found really interesting was that she said she removed any potential vows and oaths that were preventing me from fulfilling my destiny.

Thank you! I don't know what my destiny is but I bet it's awesome! Can't have anything blocking it now can I?

She also told me that it's not necessary for me to know the complete details of each of these issues she cleared as people often dwell on them. I wasn't bothered by this since I didn't really have a clue what she was talking about anyway. She went on to say she smoothed out my aura and sealed my chakras.

The next day I can honestly say I felt lighter. The weird part came when that evening I felt the need to tell Tyler I had read that birthmarks were fatal injuries from previous lives. "Like this one I said," while lifting my shirt to show him a birthmark I've had on my stomach since I was born. Except it wasn't there. I ran to the bathroom mirror, thinking, "Where the heck is it?" I looked down again, and noticed it was sort of there, but very faded. If I didn't know exactly where it was I would never have been able to see it at all. I went running down the hall to my mom's room.

"MOM! You know that birthmark on my stomach?" I asked as I lifted my shirt. "Where is it?"

She looked and said, "That's weird. It's gone. You had that since you were a baby."

I knew what had happened. The Akashic Karma Clearing healing was even more effective than I ever could have imagined. Too bad she didn't give me the details. I wondered what had happened in that previous life? I had obviously died from that injury.

The Meet Your Guidance Team Reading took a few days more to arrive. In this reading she told me the Archangels that are helping me are Archangel Raziel, Archangel Haniel and Archangel Uriel. I also have Ascended Masters assisting me and they are Lord Chiron, King Solomon and Mother Teresa.

My personal message from them was that significant abundance flows to me now! *I love getting news like that!* There was more describing who the Archangels are and what their roles are. She also included descriptions about who the Ascended Masters were when they were incarnated.

What can I say about that? Quite the arsenal of guidance I have there. I am very blessed and fortunate, there's no doubt about that. I am grateful for their support. I sure hope I don't disappoint them.

Teri also mentions in her description for this reading that our guidance team can change depending on what our needs are and where we are, at the time. So a year from now, maybe I will do the same reading again.

CHAPTER 22

Night-scare

During the Christmas holidays I took two weeks off work to write this book, catch up on my spiritual reading and learning, and spend time with family. I've kept in touch with my friends through Facebook and texting or email but otherwise I have remained secluded. My mom announced she will be moving out of our house and in with her boyfriend in Red Deer. We're all very happy for her and I have an additional reason to be excited because it means I can convert her room into an office / Reiki treatment room. I've already begun decorating it in my head. First I will paint the room a healing green colour and I will move my desk in there. I got a Selenite lamp and a chakra banner that will be perfect in that room. I have an Egyptian style blanket that will go perfect on the table I still have to get. I even wrote out the Reiki principles, so I could frame it and hang it on the wall. I'll need shelves for all my crystals so I will convert the closest into solid shelves.

Christmas dinner went great. Tyler deep fried a turkey for us, which meant I only had to cook the sides. Not exactly the Christmas traditions that I grew up with, but instead we forged our own new traditions. It's funny when you think we were never religious, yet we always celebrated Christmas, which is very much a religious holiday the way I was taught. Still, I enjoy celebrating it. I love Christmas music and decorating a tree. This year I put an angel with real feather wings on top of the tree. I love having a reason to get friends and family together, and it means Tyler and I get time off work, and Seth gets time away from school!

So all in all, no family drama, just peace and quiet, and a positive atmosphere. So far it doesn't seem like any of my spiritual gifts have developed further, yet the cards I drew daily said otherwise. All I noticed was the need for a lot of sleep and more aches and pains for no apparent reason. Here's one card I got (for the first time I might add).

Destiny Cards by Cheryl Lee Harnish said:

"Ascension: Your energetic field is in a state of change and expansion. You have begun to vibrate at higher levels as your consciousness moves more in alignment with your higher self. You are one of the forerunners working towards Ascension to raise the consciousness of the planet. The changes you are experiencing are not always comfortable, but they are necessary for your continued growth. The true beauty of your soul is beginning to show and it has a positive and uplifting effect on others."

Not always comfortable? Yes, I can vouch for that!

My family is now asking for Reiki treatments rather than me asking them. Tyler had issues with his arm and asked me to work on it. His arm hurt so much, he could barely use it, which has a lot to do with his work and the fact he has reoccurring tennis elbow. I spent as much time as I could on his arm. I would have known even if he hadn't told me that it was seriously hurting and possibly damaged. An extreme tingling sensation went right up my arms! After an hour or so he said it felt tons better and he could use it normally again. He also added a tensor bandage to protect it. I kept asking how it was feeling and he said it seemed better but if it gets bad again I am sending him to a doctor to have it x-rayed.

Seemingly out of the blue I got a call from Jessie who wanted to talk because she had been thinking about me over Christmas and wanted to chat about what happened previously when I needed that intensive healing after the Reiki II attunement. I didn't feel like chatting with her but I couldn't think of a reason not to. It was her belief that something dark had been attracted to my gifts and energy. I guess she was concerned and wanted to make sure I was better now, which I told her I was. My creative energy was flowing and I was sleeping well, other than a new pain that arose in my right hip. I asked if she knew what it might be. She thought it might have something to do with moving forward too quickly. After I hung up from her I felt shaky and strange.

That night it was just Tyler and myself as Seth had gone to his dad's for the weekend, and my mom and her boyfriend had gone back to Red Deer. We watched a few of our favourite shows. For some reason I felt like holding my Selenite wand. I'm always holding and playing with various crystals, so this was not unusual for me. When our shows were over and we went to bed, I put Selenite crystals at the four corners of our bed. Tyler asked what I was doing.

"Oh, just trying something. Selenite is supposed to be good for protection," I said. I didn't have a reason other than I felt like it.

I drifted off easily and was having pleasant dreams when something disturbed my sleep. I opened my eyes. I had been lying on my back and when I opened my eyes in that half-awake state I saw something hovering right above me! I swung out my arms, screaming, "Get away from me!" Of course, this woke Tyler but it took a few more seconds of screaming before I finally stopped and switched to shuddering.

He asked if I had a bad dream.

"No I didn't. I was having good dreams actually. I don't know WHAT that was about but I could have sworn something was there."

He comforted me and started to go back to sleep. He snores loudly, so I usually wear ear plugs but I was too scared now to NOT have all my senses on alert. I told him he was snoring and bothering me and he kindly went to sleep in the other room, so I didn't have to wear ear plugs.

Of course this created a new issue. Now I had to go back to sleep ALONE. Crap! I tossed and turned for a few minutes and knew there was no way I could sleep now but I was SO tired.

In a sad and probably whiny voice, I asked if my angels and guides could please place protection around me. And to please stay with me so that I could fall sleep.

Somehow, eventually, I drifted off again.

The next morning, I texted Colleen from work and told her what had happened. She was at home and replied immediately asking me to call her. I did right that minute. I told her everything that had happened that day. Who I spoke to, what I did, even the placing of my crystals before bed, and what I vaguely recalled happening during the night.

"Well" she started, "from what I can see it looks like something dark was attracted to you. These things know what your gifts are and they are attracted to it. These things use fear to get their hooks into you. You need to protect yourself and I cannot stress this enough," she told me firmly. "You need to place protection around yourself and your home. Do you know how to use sage to cleanse?"

"Yes," I said quietly.

"Okay, and you know to go clockwise?" she asked.

"Yes, but I didn't do it yet today" I said sheepishly.

"Okay. Whatever you use to protect yourself and your home you still need to renew it frequently."

"Okay," I replied.

"Were you talking to someone yesterday or did you meet with anyone?" Colleen asked.

"Just Jessie, my Reiki instructor on the phone," I said.

"It seems to have come from her somehow. I get it has something to do with your Reiki," Colleen said.

"Oh, well I did have that incident at her house. Maybe she's unaware there was something hovering," I said, wondering.

"I also saw your angels lying in bed with you while you slept."

I laughed. "Yes I asked them to. I was a little freaked out."

I told Tyler everything she had said and then asked if he could stop at the metaphysical store after work as I needed some supplies.

That night I used white sage to cleanse the entire upper floor. I made sure to open a window so any negative energy could leave and so the fire alarm wouldn't go off. Seth, always curious, asked what I was doing, so I told him. He watched and asked questions that I answered as best I could. I had to keep re-lighting the sage to keep enough smoke going. When I was convinced I had left no spot untouched by the sage smoke, I ran what was left under water to put it out.

Then I grabbed the sweet grass, which I was told cleanses but also blesses a space. I had trouble keeping it lit. It's possible I was doing it wrong but I kept relighting it with a candle that I had burning nearby. Then I took four pieces of Selenite, all about six inches long and placed them in the four corners of the room pointing North to South. I had to ask my ten year old which direction was North and South. I thought I knew but knowing my crappy sense of direction, I could be wrong! He confirmed what I thought was North to South, so I placed the Selenite accordingly and said the prayer I found for protection. The best part about Selenite is that it's self-cleansing and self-charging so once placed they never need to be touched ever again. I'll just say the prayer every now and again, just to be on the safe side.

Maybe it was overkill but if it meant not being woken up in the middle of the night like that again, I was willing to try pretty much anything! I had no issues that night, or the next...

CHAPTER 23

The Tattoo

Well I finally got around to purchasing that book written by Dan Millman called *The Laws of Spirit*, the one I was supposed to focus on The Law of Cycles, as Angie who did Belief Re-Patterning told me. It was the evening on December 29, 2014 and almost a New Year. It was hard to believe it had only been 120-days since this spiritual awakening began. So I settled on the couch to read. At first I thought I would read the section that Angie had mentioned, but upon reading the first paragraph I didn't think it would make a whole lot of sense and it might be completely out of context halfway through. So I figured I would read it from the beginning instead. It's not like it was a super long book anyway, so I could read it all in one night if I wanted.

My first thoughts were that it was rather abstract, making it challenging to understand at times and I reread numerous lines and paragraphs trying to grasp the point. A lot of it made total sense to me and I liked the way the Sage character explained things. Understanding these things is one thing but being able to articulate it to other people in a meaningful and non-confrontational way, is a whole other ball of wax. I was impressed by the explanations and knew I would probably be referring back to this book again later. Ten o'clock rolled around and it was time for Seth to go to bed. I decided to go up and read in bed, while Tyler stayed up quietly playing his computer game. An hour or more later I finally got to the chapter about The Law of Cycles. Seasons come and go, cycles and change (yes, yes I know all that). They must be telling me once again to be patient. I kept reading.

Then I got to the part that started, "In the ancient days, King Solomon felt great turmoil..." Whoa, wait a second. WHAT? Why are they suddenly talking about King Solomon? If you recall, King Solomon was one of my Ascended Masters according to Teri Van Horne from the Healing Light reading. So this caught my attention immediately. King Solomon just "happened" to be mentioned in the chapter I was supposed to focus on...Coincidence? Somehow I doubt it.

To directly quote the book, page 136-137:

> *"In the ancient days, King Solomon felt great turmoil,*
> *and craved the return of more peaceful times, so he*
> *decreed that a master jeweller should make him a*
> *magical ring inscribed with words that would be true*
> *and appropriate at all times and under all conditions –*
> *words that would help to alleviate suffering and provide*
> *the bearer with great wisdom and perspective. This*
> *master jeweller crafted a special ring; then, after many*
> *days' contemplation, the jeweller found the words and*
> *presented Solomon with his ring. On it were inscribed*
> *the words, 'And this too shall pass.'"*

... and the tears fell.

That's what the tattoo on my arm will be, exactly those words, 'And this too shall pass.'

Let me back up and explain.

After I got my reading from Teri Van Horne, I'll be honest, I didn't know who most of them were. The Ascended Masters, as I understood it, had all lived on Earth at one time or other but I didn't know much about them. So when free time presented itself I looked each of them up on the internet. The one that caught me by surprise was a story of King Solomon and the splitting of the baby. The reason that story caught me by surprise was because when I was six years old (before I had shut out the angels), I clearly remember flipping through a children's Bible. The book was ratty and had seen better days. I was sitting on the floor near my bedroom, all by myself, reading this book. Of all the stories in the book, the one I never forgot was the splitting of the baby. I was horrified by it truthfully! Who would suggest such a thing? Still, I liked the happy ending none the less.

The story didn't give all the gory details, but from what I remembered the story went that two women were fighting over a baby. They went to their leader to have the argument settled. The leader listened to both sides and stated that since both women believed they had claim to the child then the child would be cut in half and they each would get half of the baby. The one woman was satisfied with this, while the other screamed out, "NO! Give the baby to her. I love my child too much to see it cut in half and would rather see her have it than see my baby die." With this the leader knew who the mother was and gave the baby to the one who was willing to give the child up. Anyway I didn't remember who that "leader" was. At least not until recently when I was reading up on King Solomon to learn who he was. King Solomon was the one that suggested the baby be cut in two. He was the King from the story.

As if that weren't enough, the symbols that Teza Zialcita had drawn all over my Akashic records reading were popping up again as the "Seal of Solomon." What? I had only ever heard it called the Star of David. The very same symbol I had seen, not once but twice, on two different vehicles, and didn't know why it caught my eye. I assumed the Star of David had something to do with the clearing that was done on me during my Body Talk healing, which involved the healing on my biological father's side of that family. It seemed to fit with Teza's reading: Germany >> Jewish>>Star of David>> loss of freedom.

Now I was seeing this symbol again as the Seal of Solomon. Odd.

Anyway, now I had a vague idea who King Solomon was. He was also one of my Ascended Masters who I gather is part of a team that is going to help guide me. So of course I am going to notice when it comes up in a book, in a chapter I was supposed to read and which happened to have a quote that meant **so much to me in my life so far**. A quote I never knew had anything to do with King Solomon.

I suppose I should try to explain why that quote was and is worth tattooing on my body.

When you're young, very little is in your control. You have to rely on adults to make decisions for you and they dictate the majority of what you do, when you do it, and how you do it. Depending on the type of parents you have they may ask what you want, they may give you choices, and allow you some measure of control, even if it's as simple as being able to choose what you will wear that day. Not only did I rarely, if ever get to make decisions or choices for myself that were in my best interest, but I was also victimized in ways that a child never should be. Depending on the will of that child they may take drastic measures and fight back in a lethal way. They may commit suicide (later in life), they may resort to drugs or alcohol (again later in life), or they may internalize everything, as was the case with me. As a teenager I considered all the options at one point or another. I even considered joining the Army but figured I would be kicked out after a week due to my strong will. Where I was going with this was that the phase "and this too shall pass" were the very words that got me through it all. I do not know where I first learned that phrase, and nor do I care. When I didn't think I could possibly take any more, when I was ready to give up, I would hear the words in my head, "and this too shall pass" and I knew if I could get through today the worst would be over because nothing can last forever. Change is one thing we can always count on.

So if I was going to tattoo this quote on my arm, I wanted to see what it would look like! I typed the phase into a search engine on the internet. Naturally many people have the phrase tattooed on their bodies. I also noticed vendors selling "the ring of Solomon" with the phrase in various languages. Well, the Seal of Solomon symbol, which is also known as the Star of David, happens to be associated with that quote…

I needed to grab my pendulum because this was bugging me.

Question:
"Was I one of King Solomon's wives?"
Answer:
No.

Question:
"Is the quote 'and this too shall pass' what I was going to get tattooed on my arm?"
Answer:
Yes. (Yeah, I already knew that. I wonder if I would have thought of it if they hadn't planted the idea. I guess it doesn't matter.)

Question:
"Am I missing the point of this symbol, the Seal of Solomon?"
Answer:
"Yes" (Great, just great!)

Well I didn't know what else to ask and the stupid pendulum only answers yes or no questions, so a lot of good that does me. Maybe I'll have a brilliant epiphany in my sleep. (FYI, I didn't.)

I did spend some time on Pinterest looking for a font I liked for my tattoo. I knew the second I found it! Now the only question was, do I have it written in black ink or colour? I finally decided it had to be black because black goes with everything. Still I needed to think on it a while to be sure of where I wanted it, and to make sure I really wanted another tattoo.

CHAPTER 24

◆━━━━◆

Unexplained Phenomena

Just when I thought things couldn't get any stranger… I realized how wrong I was.

It started a few months ago but I didn't put it together right away. We seemed to be going through light bulbs in the house at a very rapid rate. I complained to Tyler that be must have bought the cheapest bulbs ever! The bulbs in the kitchen were popping almost weekly.

He said, "Cheap?! Those bulbs were $24 bucks a piece!"

Oh.

My response was, "Well then there must be something wrong with the bloody electrical wiring in this house!"

Tyler's theory was that anyone walking around upstairs must be making the bulbs shake too hard and it was causing them to burn out at an accelerated rate. That seemed reasonable to me so we went and bought extra bulbs. The problem was, it wasn't only the kitchen bulbs! Of six bulbs in the kitchen we were lucky if we had three working at any given time. The bulb in the living room, **POP!** The bulb in the dining room, **POP!** Then it occurred to me that it was only happening when "I" was the one turning on the light switch.

It wasn't until someone I knew was complaining about watches never working for them, that I started to put two and two together to make an epiphany. I've never had a watch keep its time, which is why I rarely wear them. The time either got slower and slower, or the second hand would stop moving altogether. I would change batteries, take watches to be repaired, all to no avail. Finally, I gave up. I never had the right time no matter how hard I tried. Everyone else always had a different time. Even when I got an iPhone and an iPad the time was always ten minutes different than EVERYONE else's. When I asked how to fix it I was told the time was provided by satellite, and you can't change it. I'm just not meant to know the correct time I guess.

So what if the electrical in some of us works a little differently than others? Could higher vibrations interfere with electronics? I started searching but came up with very little. Either only a select few souls were brave enough to mention it or they didn't know they were the cause. I guess it is also possible that it doesn't happen to many people and that's why there's very little information about it. Once this thought process entered my mind I paid more attention to when the bulbs burnt out. I didn't have to wait long.

One morning I was getting ready for work and I switched on the closest light to me, **POP!** There goes another one. A few days later, also in the morning I switched on the upstairs hallway light, **POP!**

"Tyler, we need more bulbs again," I said to a sleeping Tyler. "Can you pick some more up today?"

"Sure babe," he replied groggily, "but it'd help if you stopped blowing them up."

Then I heard my mom from the other room. "Why is there no power in my room? My clock is out and my lights won't come on."

I didn't blow the breaker did I? Crap! I run downstairs to check. Sure enough, I blew the breaker, which had never happened in this house before.

"Good news Tyler, you don't have to change the hallway bulb. I just blew the breaker this time," I said.

"Okay babe," he said and went right back to sleep. I thought I would get more of a reaction than that but I guess he was tired.

When he finally got around to changing the hallway bulb downstairs, we were a little surprised to find that not only was the bulb burnt out but the darn thing had separated from the base. The glass and metal part were no longer together. Was I to blame for that, too? Probably, but there was no way to know for certain.

Over Christmas vacation I seemed to have better luck. No burnt out bulbs. Tyler had to replace a breaker in the panel for the hot tub but assured me it wasn't my fault. One afternoon, I was working at my desk on my laptop. I felt I was ready to take my Akashic records attunement now so I contacted Teza Zialcita and when she agreed, we booked a time. I was so excited! I leaned over to turn on the light in my Selenite lamp for ambiance and my four day old lamp that I got for Christmas went **POP**!

"Seriously! It's brand new!" I snapped at the lamp.

I figured I would take the bulb out and see if it's one I had a replacement for, but while holding the bulb in my hand the bloody thing exploded! It didn't just break; it actually exploded with such force that it shattered glass into the tiniest pieces possible and sent them everywhere. I had to get Tyler to bring me the vacuum because if I moved I would have got shards of glass in my feet and I was standing on the carpet. It was difficult to pretend that one wasn't totally my fault. Was it just because I was so excited? I had no clue, but I wish I did because clearly I needed to learn to control this. That was almost dangerous.

One morning after that incident, I remembered something I read in Sylvia Browne's books, that the "other side" doesn't have electricity. That angels and everyone else on the "other side" are drawn to candlelight on this side. From what she said in the book they can't even see unnatural lights when visiting us, but they can see the fire of a candle. I wonder if that's because they would blow everything up due to their extremely high vibrations? Which makes me wonder, is it my visitors that are causing blown bulbs? Maybe it's not me personally at all? No answers seem to be forthcoming right now but I hope to figure it out eventually.

I have come to rely on my pendulum to answer or confirm certain question. I was told by Colleen that my guides wanted me to put it away and not to rely on it so much because I needed to learn to trust my own gifts. That would be fine if my gifts were a lot clearer! Sometimes I need a straight answer. I do try to figure things out on my own, but when I start feeling really frustrated I pick up my pendulum. So far I thought I had a good idea of what my gifts were but I wanted to confirm it and see if I had gifts I didn't know about yet.

Question: "Am I a clairaudient?"
Answer: Yes.

Question: "Am I a clairsentient?"
Answer: Yes.

Question: "Am I an empath?"
Answer: Yes.

Question: "Am I a shaman?"
Answer: No. (Darn I thought maybe I was.)

Question: "Do I currently have the ability to astral travel?"
Answer: No.

Question: "Do I currently have the ability to channel?"
Answer: Yes. (That one surprised me.)

Question: "Can I develop my ability as a clairvoyant?"
Answer: Yes.

Question: "Can I develop the ability to astral travel?"
Answer: Yes.

Question: "Can I become a Shaman?"
Answer: Yes.

I have a feeling the answer would be yes to anything I wanted to do or learn. Would I develop these abilities? How long would it take might be a better question. For now I need definitions for these terms. I didn't find any definitions that felt accurate, so instead I pieced together definitions in my own words of what they mean to me:

Clairaudient means 'Clear Hearing.' Wherein a person acquires information by paranormal auditory means.

Clairsentient means 'Clear Feeling.' Most people use clairsentience on a daily basis. This is your guides/Higher Self, sending you intuitive guidance. If you have ever had a physical or emotional feeling suddenly wash over you with no apparent connection to your current state of mind, you have just experienced clairsentience.

Clairvoyance means 'Clear Vision.' It is using the ability of the Third Eye directly so you can visually witness what is shown to you.

Channeling is communication with any consciousness that is not in human form and allowing that consciousness to express itself through a person in physical form. It is the reception of thought from the spirit world for the purpose of communicating with spirits (non-corporal entities, spirits of the deceased, or nature spirits) and angels.

Astral Travel is a spiritual interpretation of the out-of-body experience. We each possess a soul that can roam freely from the body while we are in a semi-sleep or a trance state.

I realize as I write this, that once I publish this book I will lose friends because of it but I will also gain new friends too. That reminds me of what Grandpa told me, *"Your circle of friends will change."* He's right, of course, and now I know what he meant by that. His message does bring some comfort. I know that once I come out of the spiritual closest, things will change drastically but I know in my heart I am doing it for the greater good, not for myself. It's not really about me, it's about everyone. So when the going gets tough I will look down at my arm and know, "And this too shall pass."

(While also secretly being thankful that people like me are no longer burned at the stake or stoned to death.)

CHAPTER 25

Akashic Records Activation

So what are Akashic records exactly and why would I want to activate it?

Since Teza Zialcita is my instructor I will use her definition:

"What Are Akashic Records
They are the individual Records of a soul from the time it extends from the Source until it returns. It is the Records of all your thoughts, emotions, words and deeds in the spiritual realm. The collective consciousness of all that is, the Universal Laws, and field of energy that is generated in this realm is composed of the Akasha. The energetic substance from all life is formed and records because its objective is to record all life experiences. Akasha is a Sanskrit word meaning ether or sky, primordial substance, and vibration of your soul's consciousness.

The process of accessing or opening the Records is a transition from a state of ordinary human consciousness to a state of Divine, Universal and Cosmic consciousness in which we recognize our oneness with the Divine at all levels. It allows us to perceive the impressions and vibrations of the Records' Divine illumination and integration. They are glimpses of Heaven on Earth. It affects our thoughts and emotions to begin to experience an increased sense of peace and well-being. It is protected and governed by The Lord of the Akashic Records to ensure the safety and integrity of the Records."

Now if that made sense to you then you're not new to this stuff, but for me that definition was confusing; at least at first.

Akashic records level 1 doesn't allow me to do what Teza does, which is to do readings for other people. The level 1 attunement only allows me to access my own "records" as they seem to be referred to. The way I understand it is that for as many times as you have incarnated, which is another way of saying however many lives you've lived, you generate a record of that life. That is, all the information about yourself physically, emotionally, mentally, spiritually is recorded and kept in what I will refer to as a higher plane of existence. At that higher plane of existence exists beings that protect, monitor, and access the records upon request. The tricky part is that you have to be "attuned" by an Akashic records master to access your records. Where that all started and by whom I do not know as of yet. The master essentially transfers the energy to the student and then teaches them how to access their records with the best results.

So Teza attuned me as promised, taught me the methods for opening my records, and then how to do a reading for myself. A reading basically meant asking questions and "listening" telepathically for the answer. The frustrating part is I didn't always get an answer, or if I did get an answer I didn't necessarily like the answer I got. I was told not every question will garner an answer for many reasons, but sometimes it's just how you phrase the question, so it does take practice and skill.

Teza also told me that just having my Akashic records open helps me to heal. That opening my records was not just about getting information, but also about healing myself in this life. She told me to open my records every day or at least as often as possible. The more I did it the better I would get at it because it's like working a muscle. You need to use it to get stronger.

She did say opening my Akashic records while I was writing was also beneficial because I could access information that would not normally be accessible from my conscious memory. So I did, although I didn't notice any difference so maybe it was very subtle. I did open my records a few times the first few days after my attunement but I found the answers I got more frustrating than anything, so I took a break from it sooner than I should have.

When Teza told me she was coming back to town again for a show I asked if she would give me the level 2 attunement, which allow me to access other people's Akashic records for them. Basically, I would be able to do readings for other people. I needed someone to practice on while Teza monitored so my friend Rhonda came with me. She wanted the level 1 attunement anyway so it worked out for both of us.

Once Teza did her thing and I repeated everything I was told to, it was time to open Rhonda's Akashic records. I was extremely nervous! What if it didn't work? What if I didn't get anything? Rhonda was so excited about having someone do a reading for her and I didn't want to disappoint her. It turns out I worried about nothing. I wasn't able to do a full scan like Teza wanted me to, but when Rhonda asked questions I could provide answers to most of her questions. Not all of them though. I had trouble accessing names, but I was able to get initials and that seemed to be enough. I mostly got images, no sounds or anything dramatic. Although when I smelled cigarette smoke I asked the girls if they smelled it too. They didn't and we were in a hotel room with the windows closed. Then my throat started to feel scratchy so I mentioned that. Rhonda then realized it was her grandpa and laughed because he's always checking in on her. Rhonda is a medium and is used to dead people hanging around her and talking to her but I was not. She told me her grandpa said sorry about the smoke. I heard nothing myself but after her grandpa apologized the smell went away and so did my scratchy throat.

After about ten questions I had to call it quits. The session was exhausting for me and I was having difficulty answering her last question. Nothing was coming through and I figured it was because I was too tired to focus anymore.

Unlike Reiki, which I find fairly energizing or relaxing, Akashic work required significantly more of me mentally and spiritually.

Since that day I have combined the practice of opening a person's Akashic records then channelling Reiki to them with fantastic results. I hope to do more of this in future if I have willing participants to work with. It will be interesting to see how this skill develops in the coming years with greater practice. It hasn't even been a year since my awakening yet and I'm starting to realize this is a lifelong journey. Not just a practice that you go to school for, get your certificate, and then get a job. It appears to require dedication, concentration, honing of the skill, and the desire to be of service to others. Its' humbling that anyone trusts me to do a reading for them because you truly are affecting someone's life whether they fully realize it or not.

It's not a parlour trick.

It's not a game.

CHAPTER 26

Reiki Master

Colleen and I went to a gem and crystal shop over lunch hour one day. I find myself using crystals more and more these days. Carrying them in my pockets, in my purse, using them when I do Reiki or making gem water, and generally experimenting with them to see what I can do with the energy I feel coming from them.

While I was oohing and awing over all the pretty crystals in the store, Colleen was telepathically being told to go and talk to another lady in the store and to introduce her to me, unbeknownst to me. Then Colleen introduced me to Leila. Leila and I hit it off right away and I found out she and I had the same Reiki 1 and 2 instructor. What are the chances of that? Plus, she also gave pedicures out of her home. I wanted to chat more so I booked a pedicure appointment with her and we exchanged contact information.

My appointment with Leila was inspiring. Through her I learned a little more about protecting myself and my space. She taught me a phase that I could use anytime, which goes: "This is my body, this is my space. Only my light can come from me. Only my light can come to me. Only my light can be here." Repeat three times. Certainly it wasn't enough to fully protect me and I learned that right away, however it did help if I was in a situation where my anxiety level was going up because of the people around me.

The other thing I learned from her was that the University of Mount Royal in Calgary offered Usui Reiki 1, 2, 3 and Master as well as Karuna Reiki. I still only had my Reiki level 2 and the other levels were not being offered by the person I went to for level 1 and 2, so I decided to check it out. The downside was that they didn't accept accreditation from another source, so to get my level 3 and Master, I had to retake level 1 and 2 and that meant paying for it again. I didn't mind though because different instructors teach in different ways, so I could learn a different style and it would be worth it to be accredited from a University. The bonus is that every attunement provides healing.

The university teaches Reiki 1 and 2 over two days, so on April 11 and 12, 2015 I retook my Reiki 1 and 2. I adored the instructor! She was such a kind and compassionate person. She never told anyone what was right or wrong for them. Instead, she told the class that everyone's journey is very individual and you will know what's right for you but that may not be what's right for someone else. I found her classes to be educational and informative as she shared her experiences with us. I made some friends that weekend as well. Reiki 3 and Master were over one weekend as well, and I completed both on May 29 and 30, 2015.

We are taught that after each attunement you need 21 days of doing self Reiki every day. The reason for this is that the new energy your body is adjusting to is going through each of the seven chakras and clearing them, starting at the top and working its way down each day. After seven days the cycle repeats and this happens for three cycles or three weeks. This process was very tiring for me. No matter how much sleep I got, or how healthy I ate, I felt tired. The body has to physically adjust and it can take its toll.

Something I learned when I started offering Reiki myself was that groups of people liked to get together for Reiki shares. You get a group of people together that have been attuned to any level of Reiki and you take turns doing Reiki on each other. One person will be on the table while two to four people provide Reiki for the one lying down. I thought this was brilliant, so I asked Rhonda and another Reiki practitioner Jason, whom I met through friends, if they wanted to do a Reiki share. They were excited about the idea so we set a date. That was an evening I will not forget. We all took turns and I went last. I won't speak of their sessions as they were personal, but I can say what happened for me.

My hip had been bothering me, so I asked if someone could focus on that. Then I closed my eyes, fully expecting a relaxing session. I channelled Reiki through my own hands as well, directing toward myself. Jason mentioned being able to smell campfire smoke. Rhonda had her eyes closed while concentrating. The next thing I knew, the scene had changed and I was seeing it happen in my head while I told Rhonda and Jason exactly what I was seeing.

I looked down; I was wearing a World War One uniform and I had a helmet on. I was a man in this lifetime. I felt young, early twenties I think. I appeared to be in a camp. There were soldiers all around me going about their business. I saw the campfire and everything seemed like business as usual. Then there was a huge explosion! I wondered if someone had stepped on a mine? Did I? Oh my god, my legs hurt! I was physically feeling pain in my legs in the present. "My legs, please work on my legs!" I could tell Rhonda and Jason were reacting to my distress and were trying desperately to help me. Then Rhonda was pulled into the same scene, somehow seeing what I was seeing. "It's shrapnel! I have shrapnel in my legs!" I said in the present. It felt like forever but it was probably only a few minutes and then the pain eased as Rhonda and Jason continued the Reiki. As I began to relax, I looked down in my mind's eye to see that my legs were gone from the thigh down. There were white bandages wrapped around my stumps, and that's where the scene ended.

I know without a doubt that was one of my past lives. I had been shown that scene because I needed to heal the cell memory by bringing the pain to the surface, but I guess I didn't need too many details because I have no idea what happened before or after that. Just that one traumatic scene. At least now I know why I shy away from anything related to war in this lifetime.

It seems that Reiki can trigger any number of things that need to be healed for a person but the experiences depend on what gifts we have developed and how willing we are to experience these things. The body and mind have to be willing and ready because we won't be given anything we cannot handle.

On that note I will share a few tips I picked up about when it's NOT a good idea to do Reiki on someone, keeping in mind that Reiki NEVER replaces a doctor's visit:

1. It is not suggestible to practice Reiki on someone who has broken a bone that has not been set yet. If the bone starts to heal too soon it could heal in the position it's in and needs to be re-broken to set it in the correct position. It's better to wait until a doctor has set the bone right and casted the person before practicing any Reiki on the client.

2. People with heart conditions who are on medication. The client taking the medication needs to be willing to go back to the doctor after a Reiki treatment to have their medication levels checked to make sure they are not being overdosed 'just in case' their heart issues start to improve. If they are not willing, it may not be in their best interest to share Reiki with them. The same goes for anyone on any prescribed medication. A person doesn't have to tell their doctor they got a Reiki treatment and therefore they need a check-up: it's reasonable to ask for a simple status check-up.

3. People with diabetes. If a client has diabetes and gets Reiki, advise them to check their insulin levels regularly until they've determined how the Reiki has affected them, if at all.

In any of these cases it's possible that nothing will change, but it's also possible that something could change and the client needs to be aware of the possibility. Reiki is basically supporting the body to do its own healing, so while the practitioner has no control over how their client's bodies use the Reiki energy, they still need to educate them.

CHAPTER 27

Angel Progress Update

By this point if I wasn't already totally convinced that angels were guiding me, then the next sign I got would pretty much have cemented it for me. I was driving to work, which usually take about 45 minutes to reach my destination on a typical day. No matter how fast or slow traffic is, I always have to be in the fast lane. I'm always in a hurry, even when I'm not.

It didn't take long before I happened to notice the vehicles around me were white or silver. That in itself was not unusual – at least not at first. What I did start to find odd was that no matter how many times cars around me changed lanes, sped up or slowed down, I was still surrounded by mostly white and/or silver vehicles. One white vehicle would turn off and another would take its place. This occurred the entire way to work. I justified this by thinking maybe white and silver are popular colors this year. I reached my parking spot and started walking the three blocks to my office. Every single vehicle that passed me in the lane beside where I was walking was white or silver. I'm talking, cars, trucks, work trucks, you name it.

At 10 a.m I had to leave the office and walk back to my vehicle because I had a meeting at a different location. And the same thing happened along my walk and drive to the other building! I saw a significantly increased number of white and silver vehicles. I parked in an open spot where no cars were parked close by and I ran into my meeting. When I came out there was a white vehicle parked on either side of my Toyota.

It was hard to ignore this by now. I pulled out of the lot, thinking I would go to my favorite sushi place for lunch and as I was sitting there waiting for a green light, every vehicle that passed was, you guessed it, white! Once I reached the restaurant I sat down and after placing my order I started messaging people to tell them what I'd been seeing all day and ask what the heck it meant? They suggested it was probably about moving forward and Rhonda offered to tune into the angels and ask what the message was. Meanwhile, I glanced out of the window in the moment that four white vehicles passed. I chuckled and softly thanked the angels for the signs, promising to figure out what they were trying to tell me. Then I remembered I had installed an app on my phone called "Daily Guidance from your Angels" oracle cards by Doreen Virtue.

So I pulled a card that read: "*Steady Progress. We acknowledge you for the progress you've made in remembering love in your daily activities. We can clearly see the contribution you're making to the world through your thoughts, feelings, and actions of love. You drew this card as reassurance that you're making steady progress. You sometimes harshly compare yourself to others and feel that you should be farther ahead on your path by now. Yet look how far you've come, how many lessons you've learned and how many people you've helped! Focus on your progress, instead of expecting perfection from yourself. Each day, take at least one small action step concerning a project that you're passionate about.*"

That rang so true for me at the time.

Later that day, Rhonda got back to me with her reading. Here is what she told me:

"Okay, white is Archangel Gabriel. Your angels want to let you know "we are with you." I'm seeing a white lily being presented, an older female is opening up before me. They are saying, "Don't give up, you are on the right path." They are showing me waves and I'm to tell you to go with the flow. When the tide comes in, ride it, as you will always land on your feet. Are you drinking pure water? Distilled or reverse osmosis? You are never alone. If you ever feel that way call upon them and they will appear. You will begin to notice numbers, colors, and other signs more frequently, giving you gentle nudges. Numbers are signs of the energy around you. Why have you stopped writing? They are showing me a small strip of paper with handwriting on it. You have knowledge inside that needs to be shared. Does this make sense? Look up the meaning of white lily. Love and Light."

At the time I got this message I hadn't been writing and I felt a little discouraged. I didn't have any motivation and I was having issues with finances. I hadn't been drinking water because I never do. I don't like water much. I had been seeing numbers everywhere. Usually I would look up the meaning but sometimes I forgot. The fact is, I felt a little depressed and was struggling to do the day-to-day things. I guess they recognised that I needed some support and love.

I assumed that once I got the message and acknowledged it, I would stop seeing so many white and silver vehicles, but I was mistaken. It continued for the remainder of the day. The next day everything returned to "normal."

CHAPTER 28

✦━━━━━━✦━━━━━━✦

Employed By Angels

Somewhere along the way I knew I wanted to start a healing business. I didn't know what services I would provide and I didn't know when I would start my business, but I needed a company name. I tossed a few ideas around, but nothing stuck. Then I remembered something I read in one of Doreen Virtue's books. The gist of it was that light-workers could think of themselves as working for God as if it were a business. They work for 'God Incorporated.' It made sense in a way. However, I still had/have this hang up from my days as an Atheist and I still don't like to use the word god. Anyway, that's how I came up with the name "Employed by Angels."

I started out with a Facebook page that grew fast and then maintained approximately 15 people. As always, some people lurk, some comment and post, and others hit 'like' from time to time. I felt it was a safe way to test the waters and see what kind of feedback I got. I warned my immediate family that I would be "coming out" by first telling everyone I was an empath, and then explaining what that meant. Fortunately, they were supportive, but not everyone is so lucky.

I started researching what the business license requirements were in my town for working out of my home. I had my own healing room in my house, so I figured I might as well use it. I had been using it to practice doing Reiki, past life regressions, and Akashic records readings while I built my confidence but I knew I couldn't practice forever. I had bought my own training materials and supplies, and I had invested a significant sum into training and classes, not to mention my time. I knew at some point I would have to start charging for my services. When I told my friends Rhonda and Colleen about my thoughts on starting a business they both saw a future practice. When they gave me details I had to stop them as I wanted to come up with at least SOME of the ideas on my own.

I wanted to make sure I was offering my clients everything I could, so I decided to get a Psychic Attunement from Teri Van Horn. I had experienced a lot of success with her in the past so I felt good about going to her again. The Brow Chakra is one that is most often associated with intuitive abilities and the awakening process, so for the Psychic Attunement she works with your Brow Chakra as well as the Throat and Heart Chakra to enhance your abilities to receive messages and information meant for you to access. After the session, you can expect to experience more opportunities with seeing things, hearing things, feeling or sensing things, or an overall sense of knowing. This sounded like the boost I needed before getting my business up and running so I purchased a session.

My biggest take away from that reading was that I do not have any Karmic issues or past life experiences causing me any problems at this time and that I am not under psychic attack, nor do I have any negative entities attached. Receiving that confirmation was huge for me. It told me that all the work I had done in the past 11 months, all the money I had spent, all the energy I had spent, was beneficial. Each of those issues had come up this past year. This doesn't mean new stuff won't come up but I finally reached a point where there wasn't something I had to work through. I could confidently treat clients without any concern that I might transfer any lower energies to them. I finally achieved GOOD VIBRATIONS!

CHAPTER 29

Akashic Records Weekend Workshop

Soon after starting to set up my home based business, my friend Teza contacted me about holding a workshop in my town. She would be coming from BC and wanted to see if I was interested in helping her arrange a level 1 and 2 workshop. Naturally I said, "Yes, of course!" I was totally honored to be a part of guiding others in developing their abilities, which would then in turn help many more. It was agreed that we would hold the workshop at my cottage on Ghost Lake on the August long weekend, which also happened to be the weekend of the Blue Moon. It only comes around about every 2.7 years and is energetically a more intense time. I can attest to that because the day before the workshop when the moon was at 97 percent I was having issues staying grounded. It felt like my blood sugar was low because I felt shaky, I had trouble focusing, and I was very scatterbrained, somewhat agitated, and hyper; all symptoms of not being grounded.

The reason we become ungrounded during a major astrological event like this is because the air becomes charged with positive ions, which can be disturbing to energetically sensitive people. The Earth, which normally carries a negative charge, is what helps ground us by infusing our bodies with negative ions, unless like me a person is working in an office, wearing rubber-soled shoes, and can't use the Earth to ground. In that case, I try to carry grounding crystals and drink water and eat root vegetables, which all help but don't last long for me so I had to keep working on staying grounded. At the same time, the extra boost of energy makes doing energetic work like the Akashic records workshop much more intense.

The workshop itself was a lot more work than I thought. I knew it would be energetically intense, so I knew I would be very tired at the end of both days, but there was a lot of prep work involved as well. Not only for shopping, prepping food, arranging the room, clearing the room, and making sure we had training materials, but also my own energy having the Akashic records open and being connected to everyone in the room. I had a major headache at the end of both days. When Teza opened the Akashic records for everyone in the room I felt a slight pressure on the top of my head and a tingling sensation and warmth moved down as far as my nose. That eventually turned into a headache. When Teza closed the records it was an almost immediate relief yet the headache, while less intense, remained until I had fully rested.

The amazing people in the workshop opened up, shared, released, and grew before my eyes. On the second day of the workshop I paired up with someone to allow them to do an Akashic record reading for me to practice. While she was doing that I was tuning into myself as well. When I did a scan of my body I got a pain in the middle to right side of my chest but I didn't understand why so I asked Teza to tune into me. She said, "Oh it's a past life thing that came up, but it's not something you need to heal from today. You were sacrificed on a table in a ceremonial sacrifice."

"Why am I not surprised?" I said. Since I was a healer in many lifetimes before it's a sure bet that I died at the hands of others in many disturbing ways simply for being what I am.

A different topic of discussion came up during the workshop that had nothing to do with Akashic records, but the word Star Seed was mentioned and everyone wanted to know what it meant and if it applied to them.

According to the website Sirius Temple of Ascension by Paul McCarthy http://www.siriusascension.com/what%20is.htm:

"Star Seeds are beings that have experienced life elsewhere in the Universe on other planets and in non-physical dimensions other than on Earth. Star Seeds may also have had previous life times on earth.

Common characteristics of all Star Seeds:

A deep interest in spirituality
The ability to spiritually grow rapidly when needed as if they have done this before
A realization that earth is not their true home
They feel drawn to outer space, the stars, and science fiction
Personal qualities such as being artistic, being sensitive, and possessing higher consciousness
Star Seeds can have difficult and challenging lives
They sometimes have dreams or memories of places not on earth
They sometimes have experiences of physical and non-physical encounters with star guides and UFOs
They often have noticeable gifts in the areas of healing, channeling, and psychic sensitivities."

Their website does go further into detail and I have found a few books written on the subject, such as *Starseeds* by Louis Edward Alfeld and *I am a Sirian: Starseeds on Earth!* by The Abbotts.

Based on all the feedback we received, the workshop was a success! I was proud of the work we did and felt more convinced than ever that I am here to learn as much as possible about different healing modalities and pass that information on to others. As tiring as it is, I am passionate about this work and it feels like my calling. I know where I am going, even if I don't how exactly how I am going to get there. I still have a lot to learn, but I want to share everything I learn as I go.

CHAPTER 30

One year Anniversary

It has been a year now since my awakening as an empath. I feel that this anniversary marks the end of this book. My journey over this past year has been many things for me; intimidating, exciting, emotional, the end of some relationships, and the beginning of others, but most of all it has been the start of something amazing. I recently came to realize that my wedding to Tyler will take place on the very same day as the anniversary of my awakening, September 6, 2015. It's funny that it took me nearly a year to realize that, and it was unintentional on my part. Another coincidence perhaps? I can't say that I believe in coincidences anymore, however I can say that I finally believe in something greater than myself. When I asked for proof or some tangible evidence, I got it. It's true that the proof I was given was for me and me alone and I can only share my experience with you, but people will believe what they want to believe. I still do not feel the need to prove myself to anyone. I know who I am and what I am, and I am confident in myself and my abilities. I am well aware of how blessed I am, how gifted I am, and how fortunate I am to have been given these gifts. I may have been pushed kicking and screaming into my awakening, but I don't regret a single day of it. There is power in knowing where I came from and feeling the Truth of everything I learned about myself.

Seek and ye shall find. No one person gave me all the answers. We are not born with a manual. There isn't even a manual to being an empath and there never will be because we have freewill. We are here to make the human experience our own. It's in the seeking that we truly find the answers that are right for us. You are master of your fate; your choices led you to where you are now. If you don't like where you are now, make a different choice. To say you don't have a choice, is a choice in itself because you are choosing to do nothing. Once I understood this and accepted responsibility for my actions and choices my view of the world changed too. The only thing that is constant is change, so we can either fight it or we can go with the flow. As I look back I can see that fighting it didn't really change the outcome; it only prolonged it.

I hope I was able to show everyone that it's not always easy or smooth and there are ups and downs but I believe we appreciate our gifts more because we have to work for it. My life is not perfect. Very little has changed outside of me since I embarked on this path. What changed was me, my perceptions, my attitude, my willingness to be happy, my self-awareness, and how I make decisions. I have a long road ahead of me, yet as a mother, as a spiritual being, and as a human being, I say, BRING IT ON!

Dear reader, whatever your reasons were for choosing to read my book, I know you were meant to read it. I hope you found what you were looking for and I wish you all the blessings you deserve.

Love and Light...

EMPATH STARTER KIT

Every newly awakened empath needs a starter kit to get them started on their spiritual journey of enlightenment and support. To aid you on your path I came up with some necessities that includes a selection of items that can be used by anyone, along with instructions to get you underway. These items can be purchased at your local metaphysical store.

Item 1
My Book "Waking up and Empath" by Kim Wuirch ☺

Item 2
Quantity 1 bag or bundle: White Sage

White sage works best when burned and is used to clear away lower energy. When lit, let it burn for a few seconds and then blow the flame out and it will continue to smolder and will eventually go out. It may need to be re-lit during use. Be sure to use a fire safe dish to collect the ashes. Always open a window so that you don't set the fire alarm off and to allow the energy somewhere to go. Traditions say to walk in a clockwise motion around the room. You can also burn it in a dish and set it in the middle of a room. Use the smoke to clear rooms, your own body and spiritual items such as crystals and oracle cards. Sage is a low cost item.

Item 3
Quantity 1: Quartz Crystal Pendulum

Pendulums can be used to answer yes or no questions. Quartz Crystal is a high vibration and versatile crystal. It can easily be used by anyone. A pendulum is simply a crystal with a point that has a chain attached to it. Quartz is common and should be a low cost item.

Instructions for use:

1. Rinse your crystal under cold water to start the clearing process. Using some burning sage hold the crystal in the smoke for at least one minute to clear any remaining energies from others handling it in the store.
2. Now it's ready to absorb your energy. Hold the crystal in your hand for at least half an hour or carry in your pocket for half a day. There is no right or wrong amount of time.
3. To attune the pendulum to you rest your elbow on the table and hold the top of the chain between your thumb and pointer finger. Make sure the crystal is not touching the table and is at rest (no movement). Keeping your arm steady ask to be shown a Yes. The direction it swings is a **Yes** for you. *(This will differ from person to person.)* With your other hand stop the movement. When it's at a full stop, keeping your arm steady ask to be shown a **No**. The direction it swings is a No for you. With your other hand stop the movement. When it's at a full stop, keeping your arm steady ask to be shown a Maybe. The direction it swings is a **Maybe** for you.
    If you got no response simply allow more time for the pendulum to attune to you.
4. Now that you know the direction it will give you for each answer, you can ask a question. Start with something you already know the answer to such as the name of a pet. Try using a fake name, once you get your answer stop it and try the real name.

5. Now you can ask your questions. Be aware that if you ask too many questions you may start to get false answers or no answers at all. If your guides feel you are abusing the pendulum or becoming too reliant on it they will interfere with the results.

Item 4

Quantity 1: Tiger Iron

Tiger Iron is a wonderful grounding crystal. There are many other options for crystals that can help you ground but Tiger Iron is my favorite. Choose at least one to carry in your pocket with you. Preferably a polished stone so that it's comfortable to be in your pants pocket. The closer it is to you the better it will work. Purchase multiple and you can have one in your jacket, purse and near your bed at all times. Tiger Iron is a low cost item.

Item 5

Quantity 1 bag: Epson Salts or sea salt
Quantity 1: Lavender Essential oil *(check for skin sensitivity before use)*

This is optional but recommended. At least once a week have a bath with one cup of Epson Salts or Sea Salt and 3-6 drops of lavender oil (depending on size of tub). It will help to cleanse your body of lower energies and ground you with the added benefit of being very relaxing. It's also a great opportunity to practice meditation. An all in one solution!

Item 6

Quantity 1: A box of tissues

We all know how sensitive we empaths are! A box of tissues is a staple item. ☺

RECOMMENDED EXERCISES

Journaling

For all new empaths and anyone going through a spiritual awakening I highly recommended that you start journaling immediately.

Record your dreams because they disappear quickly and you may need extra time to figure them out. Pay particular attention to dreams with strong emotions associated with them. These may have special meaning for you. Or your subconscious is trying to give you a message.

Write down any significant experiences even if you do not know what they mean yet. Over time when you look back you may start to see patterns. Jot down a line or two or a whole page. It doesn't matter how much you write. Type it out if you want. Capture your feelings and thoughts or draw if you have that skill.

Write down your spiritual experiences. If you did not have any that day then write down how your day went. Delve into where you are at emotionally.

Often times we heal through the action of expressing ourselves through our writing, paintings and drawings. Maybe you will even turn it into a blog or a book.

Grounding/Earthing

Use any combination of these techniques to ground your energy. I suggest that you try each one at least once to determine what works best for you. You may need more than one of these techniques depending on who you are with and what you are doing throughout the day. Always ground yourself before and after doing any spiritual work. Be prepared to do this at least once a day, potentially more if required:

- Earthing. This means walking in the grass barefoot, letting your body come in contact with the Earth by laying down on the ground. You can also sit against a tree with your back to the tree. Go for a picnic and make an afternoon of it!
- Salt Water. Salt and water separately are great for grounding the bodies energies but combined they are much more powerful. Go for a swim in the ocean if that's an option. If not, have a salt bath. You can use whatever salt you have in the house or even baking soda but my preference is Epson salts or sea salts. Feel free to add some essential oils to that bath (smells nice too)!
- Grounding crystals. My favorite is Tiger Iron but there are many grounding crystals. Just walk into any metaphysical store and ask for grounding crystals and they will be more than happy to point out a selection of crystals. Use your intuition to choose the right one or just grab whichever one you favor the most. Carry them in your pocket close to your body or at least nearby in a purse or jacket. When extra grounding is needed just hold it in your hand.
- Visualization. I'll give you two but you can use any visualization that feels right for you. Picture yourself with tree roots coming out of your feet and growing into the ground. Feel yourself being pulled down and anchored, rooted to the spot. Or imagine a black cord coming out of your Root Chakra going into the ground through the dirt, rocks and everything till it gets to the center of the earth. Now wrap that cord around the center of the earth and then bring back to your Root Chakra and see it being tied off there.

Cleansing away lower energy

Watch for possible signs of Lower Energy in your body and/or auric field (includes but not limited to):

- Upon waking, you feel unhappy for no particular reason.
- Lethargy, lack of energy, fatigued.
- Inability to feel upbeat or positive throughout the day.
- If you are someone who channels messages (like a psychic) you will find it more difficult to communicate as it will be fuzzy or foggy. The messages will lack clarity.
- If you are someone who channels energy (like Reiki) you will find you are channeling less energy than usual. You may feel "blocked".

Use any of the following techniques to clear your body of lower energy:

- Sage Smudging. When burning sage, make sure the smoke touches all of you, including the bottoms of your feet. You can keep your clothes on for this one! Make sure you open a window so your fire alarm doesn't go off. Sage can be found at any metaphysical store. White sage is my favorite. You can also burn sage in your home to clear the energy of each room.
- Salt baths with a few drops of lavender essential oil. Make sure you are not sensitive to lavender before putting it in your bath. Epson salts are fine too, approx. 1 cup. You might want to remove your clothes for this one!
  - o Optional ideas for the bath: Add crystals that are ok to be near water, around the edge of your bathtub. Add candles for ambiance and use this opportunity to meditate.
- Grounding (Earthing) with the intention of releasing lower energy. You should be outside for this, ideally touching the ground or a tree. Even better if you can be barefoot. Then you visualize yourself releasing all lower energy through the

palms of your hands and bottoms of your feet into the ground. Give the lower energy a color to make it easier.

- o Alternatively, if you have to remain indoors you can do just the visualization and release the energy through your hands and feet.

Meditation Exercise

Find somewhere comfortable to sit. Do not lie down unless you have back issues because you will probably fall asleep if you do. Sit against a wall, couch or a tree to support you. You can even try doing this while in a bath. For this particular meditation you need to have your eyes closed. Try to wear loose comfortable clothing and do not allow pets or children in the room with you if possible.

Read this exercise until you feel you have the steps memorized, it does not have to be exact to work. Do not be concerned if the scenes change or if you have "visitors", just relax and allow.

You start your journey in a forest. There is a pathway that is easy to see and follow so you begin your hike. So relaxed and calm you are as you walk along in this perfect temperature. Trees brush up against you as you pass. You smell the earth and local vegetation and it awakens your senses. As you continue along your guides may have joined you. Maybe your totem animal. Or perhaps this journey is just for you today.

You continue to move forward until you see a large rock that indicates where you step off the path and into your sanctuary. A place only for you. A private and safe place. Today it appears to you as a grassy clearing with a pond nearby. A small waterfall feeds the pond with clear pure water. The sound of the water falling is music to your ears. So familiar and comforting. Will you swim today? Will you wade into the pond or will you sit on the bank and dip your toes in? Will today be the day you run and jump in or sit in the grass and ponder? The choice is yours.

You can do whatever you desire in your safe haven. For here you know it's safe to ask your guides or totem animal to join you. Here you can be alone and know that you can have peace and quiet and just rejuvenate.

You spend your time here however you choose and when it's time to go, when your time is up for this moment you say good bye to your sanctuary knowing that you will be back. Back to the large rock that indicates the exit now. You follow the same path home bringing with you all the peace and love you found in that place.

REFERENCES

Crystals

Amethyst
Black Tourmaline
Blue Celestite
Blue Obsidian
Fire Agate
Moonstone
Rose Quartz
Selenite
Yellow Citrine

Lamps

Salt lamp: Salt crystal lamps are natural ion generators, emitting negative ions into the atmosphere. Negative ions restore and neutralize air quality.

Selenite Lamp: Selenite is a high vibration crystal that constantly recharges itself and can help charge other crystals that are close to it.

Definitions

("chakra." YourDictionary)
chak·ra

in certain forms of yoga, traditional Asian medicine, etc., any of a number of points in the human body, usually seven, that are considered centers of physical or spiritual energy: see chi

("reiki." YourDictionary)
Rei·ki
an alternative healing technique thought by some to reduce stress, pain, etc. through the transfer of a certain kind of energy from the hands of a practitioner to parts of the body of a person suffering from such symptoms

("aura." YourDictionary)
au·ra
noun

1. an invisible emanation or vapor, as the aroma of flowers
2. a particular atmosphere or quality that seems to arise from and surround a person or thing: enveloped in an *aura* of grandeur

a field of energy thought by some to emanate from all things in nature and to be visible to certain persons with psychic powers

Clairaudient means 'Clear Hearing.' Wherein a person acquires information by paranormal auditory means.

Clairsentient means 'Clear Feeling.' Most people use clairsentience on a daily basis. This is your guides/Higher Self, sending you intuitive guidance. If you have ever had a physical or emotional feeling suddenly wash over you with no apparent connection to your current state of mind, you have just experienced clairsentience.

Clairvoyance means 'Clear Vision.' It is using the ability of the Third Eye directly so you can visually witness what is shown to you.

Channeling is communication with any consciousness that is not in human form and allowing that consciousness to express itself through a person in physical form. It is the reception of thought from the spirit world for the purpose of communicating with spirits (non-corporal entities, spirits of the deceased, or nature spirits) and angels.

Astral Travel is a spiritual interpretation of the out-of-body experience. We each possess a soul that can roam freely from the body while we are in a semi-sleep or a trance state.

Readings

Teri Van Horne from Healing Light; http://www.healinglightonline.com/ Teza Zialcita from Akashic Soul Healing; http://akashic-soul-healing.com/

Healing Modalities

Belief Re-Patterning
Body Talk
Reiki (Usui)
Akashic Records

Other References

White Sage for smudging and cleansing home and body.
Metaphysical stores to find spiritual products such as crystals, books, sage and natural products.
Crystal singing bowls – for sound healing. Helps to balance the chakras and remove blockages.
Tibetan singing bowl – for sound healing. Helps to balance the chakras.

ABOUT THE AUTHOR

Kim was born an old woman, wise beyond her years as her mother would like to say. Yet it has served her well. Kim grew up well below the poverty line but persevered, got an education and reached her highest goals in the IT business. Then her life was turned upside down when she woke up as an Empath. Since then, she has re-educated herself in spiritualty (not religion) and set 'higher' goals. She is now guiding others through her writing, workshops and coaching. Spirituality is her passion and focus. It's time now for her to venture out, share her story and make her mark on the world.

Visit her blog at http://www.kimwuirch.com for more information, articles, videos and upcoming projects.

To see her amusing and quirky take on meditation or to learn about Advanced Chakra Energy Work check out her YouTube video channel at www.kimwuirch.com/videos

BIBLIOGRAPHY

"aura." YourDictionary, n.d. *http://www.yourdictionary.com/aura*. 18 November 2016. Web. 18 November 2016.

"chakra." YourDictionary, n.d. *http://www.yourdictionary.com/chakra*. 18 November 2016. Web. 18 November 2016.

"reiki." YourDictionary, n.d. *YourDictionary http://www.yourdictionary.com/reiki*. 18 November 2016. Web. 18 November 2016.

Abbotts, The. *I am a Sirian: Starseeds on Earth!* Lulu.com, 2012. Ebook.

Alfeld, Louis Edward. *Starseeds*. BookBaby, 2013. Ebook.

Broederlow, Chistel. *30 Traits of an Empath (How to know if you are an empath)*. 24 October 2013. Website. 5 September 2014.

Doreen Virtue, Radleigh Valentine. "Archangel Power Tarot Cards." Lifestyles, 2013. Card Decks.

Gahlin, Lucia. *Egypt - Gods, Myths and Religion*. Anness, 2001. Hard Cover.

Gienger, Joachim Goebel and Michael. *Gem Water*. Earthdancer Books, 2008. Softcover.

141

Gregg, maintained by David. *Soul Types (The Michael Teaching collective)*. n.d.

Hall, Judy. *The Crystal Bible*. Worldwide: Walking Stick Press, 2003. Paperback.

Harnish, Cheryl Lee. "Path of the Soul, Destiny Cards." Spirit's Way Designs, 1 June 2007. Cards.

Harrison, Sylvia Browne & Lindsay. *Past Lives, Future Healing*. NAL; Reprint edition, 2002. Paperback.

Hay, Louise. *Heal Your body*. Hay House; 4th ed. edition, 1984. Paperback.

McCarthy, Paul. *Sirius Temple of Ascension*. n.d. Wesbite. 2014.

Millman, Dan. *The Laws of Spirit: A Tale of Transformation*. HJ Kramer/New World Library; New edition edition, 2001. Paperback.

Phelan, Ravynne. "Messenger Oracle." Llewellyn Publications; Crds/ Pap edition, 8 May 2013. Cards.

Singer, Michael A. *The Untethered Soul: The Journey Beyond Yourself*. New Harbinger Publications; 1 edition, 2007. Paperback.

Stein, Diane. *Essential Reiki: A Complete Guide to an Ancient Healing Art*. Crossing Press; 1 edition, 1995. Paperback.

Tan, Enoch. n.d.

Virtue, Doreen. *Angels Numbers 101*. Hay House, 2008. Paperback.

—. "Daily Guidance from your Angels Oracle Cards." Hay House, 2006. Cards.

—. *Earth Angels*. Hay house, 2002. Paperback.

Walsch, Neale Donald. *Conversations with God: An Uncommon Dialogue Book 3*. Hampton Roads Pub Co, 2003. Paperback.

—. *Conversations with God; An Uncommon Dialogue Book 1*. TarcherPerigee, 1996. Hardcover.

—. *Conversations with God; An Uncommon Dialogue Book 2*. Hampton Roads Publishing Company; 1st edition, 1997. Hard Cover.

Wauters, Ambika. *The Complete Guide to Chakras*. Barron's Educational Series, 2010. Hardcover.

Zialcita, Teza. *Universal Conscious Self - simple steps to connect to your true essence*. Balboa Press, 2013. Softcover.

INDEX

M

meditate 19, 87, 131
meditation 19, 38, 87, 88, 127, 132, 139
Meditation 19, 132
medium 53, 108
metaphysical 8, 9, 14, 16, 26, 95, 125, 130, 131
moods xiii, 5, 30
Moonstone 15, 16, 135

N

negative 9, 10, 14, 31, 32, 83, 84, 86, 95, 118, 119, 135
night terrors 10
numbers 34, 35, 36, 116
numerology 21, 53, 54

O

Obsidian 56
old soul 25, 28
oracle 16, 50, 115, 125
Oracle 46, 47
out-of-body experience 105, 137

P

paranormal 2, 105, 136
Paranormal 1
peer pressure 23, 24
pendulum 25, 26, 27, 28, 29, 41, 43, 49, 66, 100, 103, 126, 127
permission 80, 84
Pisces 21, 55, 72
practitioner 38, 39, 41, 42, 112, 113
pregnant 40, 41, 59
psychic 53, 118, 121, 131

Q

Quartz 9, 126, 135
quiz 3, 4

R

realities 56
Reiki 19, 20, 38, 39, 40, 42, 43, 57, 58, 65, 66, 73, 74, 75, 76, 77, 78, 79, 80, 81, 82, 83, 91, 92, 93, 94, 108, 109, 110, 111, 112, 113, 118, 131, 137
Reiki shares 111
reincarnate 25
Religion 3
resonating 2
root 18, 120

S

sage 9, 10, 15, 94, 95, 125, 126, 131, 137
salt rock lamp 14
sea salts 130
Selenite 14, 91, 93, 95, 103, 135
sensitive xiv, 7, 21, 81, 119, 121, 127, 131
signs 11, 21, 34, 44, 115, 116, 131
singing bowls 59, 137
Sirians 51
Sirius 51, 121
Smudging 131
Soul 22, 23, 48, 49, 54, 137
Spirit 13, 52, 54, 84, 96
spirit guides 13, 14, 15, 16, 17, 27, 34, 46, 47, 63
spiritual ix, x, 6, 11, 14, 27, 49, 51, 53, 62, 63, 65, 79, 91, 92, 96, 105, 106, 123, 125, 129, 130, 137
spiritualty 139
Subconsciously 41
symptoms 7, 11, 40, 65, 119

T

tattoo 43, 97, 99, 100
telepathically 107, 110
timelines 56
totem 29, 44, 45, 60, 77, 132
Tourmaline 9, 135
toxins 40
traits 3, 4, 7, 21, 44, 49
transient 24
trauma 6, 88

U

Universal 56, 106
Universe 11, 34, 36, 63, 121
Usui 111, 137

V

vegans 6, 63

vegetarians 6, 63
veil 45
vibration 10, 11, 49, 53, 62, 63, 70, 71, 106, 126, 135
Vibration 62
Vibrations 64
Violence xiv, 5
Visualization 130

W

Wisdom 54
workshops 139

Y

Yellow Citrine 16, 32, 135
YouTube 19, 42, 139

Z

zodiac 21

Printed in the United States
By Bookmasters